Coxcomb Mtns.

177

Old Dale Rd.

...to Basin

Black Eagle Mine Rd.

...s.

Eagle Mtns.

10

Sonoran Desert

JOSHUA TREE
THE COMPLETE GUIDE

ISBN 13: 978-0-9825172-3-9

Written & Photographed
by James Kaiser

This book would not have been possible without the help of many generous people. Special thanks to Joe Zarki, Melanie Spoo, Michael Vamstad, and the entire staff at Joshua Tree National Park. Thanks also goes out to Carrie Petree, Adam Himoff, Bryan Beasley, Scott Braman, Adam Preskill, and Natalie Stone.

As always, a very special thanks to my family & friends, & to all the wonderful people I encountered while working on this guide.

All information in this guide has been exhaustively researched, but names, phone numbers, and other details do change. If you encounter a change or mistake while using this guide, please send an email to changes@jameskaiser.com. Your input will improve future editions of this guide.

Additional Photography & Image Credits
National Park Service: page 88, 91, 97, 100, 104, 107, 112, 114
Wildlife Stock Photos: page 74, 75, 77, 78, 80, 81, 84, 85; Corbis: 119
North Wind Picture Archives: page 93; NASA: page 59, 144
Printed in China

JOSHUA TREE

• THE COMPLETE GUIDE •

4th Edition

JAMES KAISER

CONGRATULATIONS!

IF YOU'VE PURCHASED this book, you're going to Joshua Tree. Perhaps you're already here. If so, you're in one of the most amazing natural landscapes in America.

Joshua Tree is beautiful. Joshua Tree is grotesque. Joshua Tree is peaceful, crazy, crowded, empty, freezing, sweltering, and a million other contradictions rolled into one. Some people think it's a wasteland. Others love it at first sight. The park lures everyone from elderly wildflower watchers to youthful rock climbers. It's a land of desert adventure packed into a landscape fit for Dr. Seuss—twisted trees and balanced boulders speckling the spectacular scenery. Add a fresh blanket of snow and you might as well be in Whoville.

And now ... my confession: The first time I came to Joshua Tree, I hated it. I was camping with friends who invited me on short notice, and we got caught in a winter storm. I had no warm clothes, it was freezing cold, and our fire kept sputtering out. If the park was like Whoville, I was like the Grinch, with grouchy complaints flowing from a mouth that was definitely not two sizes too small. On the second night, my friend's puppy, Sadie, woke up in the middle of the night, climbed onto my friend's sleeping bag, and relieved herself on his face. For my money, that premeditated piddle made the entire trip worthwhile. But otherwise the trip was a bust. By the time we left, I had no love for Joshua Tree National Park.

Thankfully, I gave the park a second chance. I came back in the early spring, when the temperature was mild, and immediately experienced a change of heart. The scenery grew on me. The strange plants fascinated me. But the real revelation came at night, when billions of stars blazed overhead. I was hooked. And I've been hooked ever since. To those of you who have ever gone to Joshua Tree and gotten lost in the stars, this book is for you.

CONTENTS

ADVENTURES (P.21)

Hiking, rock climbing, scenic drives, horseback rides—Joshua Tree is packed with desert adventure!

BASICS (P.28)

Essential park info including fees, visitor centers, campgrounds, ranger programs, weather, hazards, and more.

NEARBY TOWNS (P.37)

Tasty restaurants, funky inns, and an art scene nurtured by local hippies, hipsters, & hillbillies. Revel in the High Desert's weird and wonderful attractions.

GEOLOGY (P.47)

Learn about the powerful forces that sculpted Joshua Tree over millions of years, creating one of the most surreal landscapes in North America.

ECOLOGY & WILDLIFE (P.55)

Straddling the boundary of the Mojave and Sonoran Deserts, Joshua Tree is home to hundreds of fascinating plants and animals that coexist in remarkable ways.

HISTORY (P.89)

For thousands of years Joshua Tree was home to small bands of desert Indians. In the late 1800s gold miners and outlaws arrived. The land was federally protected in 1936, and by the end of the 20th century Joshua Tree was an internationally famous rock climbing destination.

MOJAVE DESERT (P.123)

The most famous part of the park, home to fantastic boulder formations and vast Joshua Tree forests. Spend a day or two exploring the Seussian scenery.

SONORAN DESERT (P.187)

Characterized by low elevations and high temperatures, this expansive desert seems barren at first, but it's filled with fascinating sights and beautiful destinations.

INTRODUCTION

STRADDLING THE BOUNDARY between the Mojave and Sonoran Deserts in Southern California, Joshua Tree is home to some of America's most strange and surreal scenery. The park's twisted trees, towering rock formations, and jumbled geology create a Seussian landscape that lures rock climbers, rock stars, and desert aficionados from around the globe.

At 800,000 acres, Joshua Tree takes up a vast chunk of the Southern California desert. But only two major roads run through the park: Park Boulevard and Pinto Basin Road. Park Boulevard passes through the famous Mojave Desert. Lying above 3,000 feet in elevation, the Mojave Desert in Joshua Tree occupies a slightly cooler climate filled with strange rock formations and thousands of Joshua trees. The rock formations, some as tall as twenty-story buildings, lure a steady stream of rock climbers from around the world. Joshua Tree's 8,000 plus climbs make it one of North America's premier climbing destinations—especially in the winter months when other rock climbing meccas are covered in ice and snow.

Pinto Basin Road passes through the Sonoran Desert, which is characterized by lower elevations, hotter temperatures, less rainfall, and wide-open spaces. In Joshua Tree, much of this open space lies within Pinto Basin, a 200-square-mile gulf of land that marks one of the westernmost edges of the Sonoran Desert. Pinto Basin is massive—five of the park's six mountain ranges define its boundaries. Located just a few miles north of sprawling Coachella Valley (one of the fastest growing regions in California), Pinto Basin offers a pristine reminder of the beauty of the untouched desert. Joshua trees are noticeably absent, but equally fascinating plants such as cholla, ocotillo and smoke trees call Pinto Basin home.

Several thousand years ago, Pinto Basin was settled by early Indians. The park was later used as a seasonal home by the Serrano and Cahuilla tribes. In the mid-1800s, cattle ranchers came to Joshua Tree, followed by gold miners in the 1880s. By the 1920s, however, most of the gold in Joshua Tree had been extracted, the Indians had been forced out, and only a few hardy white settlers remained. Following the introduction of the automobile, adventurous Los Angeles citizens began day-tripping to the desert in large numbers. By 1936 Joshua Tree National Monument was established. In 1994 the Desert Protection Act upgraded Joshua Tree to national park status and added 234,000 acres to its holdings. Today Joshua Tree National Park sees over 1 million visitors each year.

JOSHUA TREE
~ TOP ~
ATTRACTIONS

126 Hidden Valley — This secret valley, surrounded by towering rocks, was used as a hideout by cattle rustlers in the 1800s.

142 Keys View — Bask in panoramic views of Palm Springs and Coachella Valley from one of the highest points in the park.

174 Ryan Mountain — A dramatic hike that offers sweeping views in the heart of Joshua Tree.

180 49 Palms Oasis — This gorgeous palm oasis, reached by a moderate trail, is one of the finest destinations in the park.

62

210

Cottonwood

10

191   **Arch Rock Nature Trail** — Stroll among fantastic
      boulder formations en route to a dramatic natural stone arch.

196   **Cholla Cactus Garden** — This magnificent garden of
      multi-colored cacti is one of the most surreal sights in the park.

210   **Lost Palms Oasis** — Hike to this "lost" palm oasis, nestled
      in a remote canyon and reached by a 3.5-mile trail.

Mojave Desert

Wonderland of Rocks

Claret Cup Cactus

Winter Storm

Ryan Mountain

HIKING &
BACKPACKING

JOSHUA TREE IS a desert hiker's paradise. From easy walks to rugged multi-day backpacks, the variety of trails here is divine. Looking for exceptional views? The park boasts ten peaks greater than 5,000 feet. Enchanted by lush destinations? Head to one Joshua Tree's five gorgeous fan palm oases. Feel like a relaxing stroll? Nine easy nature trails wander through the park's famous scenery.

Hiking is the best way to experience the park. The views from your car are great, but only when you set out on foot will you truly appreciate the beauty of the desert. It's hard to enjoy a singing songbird or a blooming cactus when they're whizzing past you at 30 miles per hour. Take the time to step out of your car and you will be rewarded. But before you hit the trail, there are some important things that you need to know.

Hiking in the desert poses a unique set of challenges. Dehydration is by far the greatest concern. Joshua Tree's hot daytime temperatures and dry climate can rob you of moisture fast, so you should always carry plenty of water. A good rule of thumb is to carry at least one gallon of water per person per day when hiking long distances. Sunglasses and sunscreen are also essential, and always be aware of potential dangers such as abandoned mines, rattlesnakes, and flash floods (see page 31).

Joshua Tree has plenty of great day hikes on established trails (see page 23 for my personal favorites), but if you're looking for a more rugged adventure you can plan an overnight backpack in the backcountry. Roughly 585,000 of the park's 794,000 acres are designated wilderness, making Joshua Tree one of California's premier desert backpacking destinations.

Backpacking is a great way to explore remote sections of the park. And if you find yourself cursing the crowds and noise at established campgrounds, a quiet night in the backcountry could be right up your alley. Just follow the rules on the following page and bring plenty of water. And remember: summer days are scorching hot and winter nights often dip below freezing, so pack accordingly. Also be prepared for a wide range of conditions. Temperature changes of 40 degrees within 24 hours are not uncommon in the desert.

BACKPACKING IN JOSHUA TREE

REGISTRATION

Overnight hikers must register at one of the park's 13 backcountry boards (see inside cover map). Overnight parking is only allowed at backcountry boards.

WATER

All water sources in the park are reserved for wildlife. You must carry in all water for drinking, cooking, and hygiene. Rangers recommend at least one gallon of water per person per day for drinking.

CAMPSITES

Campsites must be located at least one mile from the road and at least 500 feet from any trail. Camping is not allowed in Day Use Areas (indicated on the maps at backcountry boards).

CAMPFIRES

Campfires are not allowed in the backcountry.

TRASH/HUMAN WASTE

All trash must be packed out. Bury all human waste in a hole at least six inches deep, but pack out all toilet paper.

JOSHUA TREE'S BEST HIKES

★ ★ ★ ★ ★

NATURE TRAILS

Arch Rock..........................191
Cap Rock............................139
Cholla Cactus Garden......................196
Cottonwood............................207
Hidden Valley........................126
High View............................171
Indian Cove..........................169
Oasis of Mara........................165
Skull Rock..........................161

Arch Rock Nature Trail

EASY HIKES

Barker Dam..........................133
Desert Queen Mine............................147
Lucky Boy Vista....................147
Pine City............................147
South Park Peak....................171
Wall Street Mill....................134

Ryan Mountain

MODERATE HIKES

Boy Scout Trail....................178
Lost Palms Oasis....................210

Mastodon Peak

STRENUOUS HIKES

49 Palms Oasis....................180
Lost Horse Mine....................176
Ryan Mountain......................174
Mastodon Peak......................208
Warren Peak........................182

Boy Scout Trail

Rock Climbing

WITH OVER 8,000 known climbs, Joshua Tree is one of the world's premier rock climbing destinations. The park's vast array of boulders and rock formations offers an astonishing range of climbs, luring everyone from total beginners to famous superstars.

Climbers first discovered Joshua Tree several decades ago. As climbing surged in popularity in the 1970s and 1980s, word leaked out about a strange place in the desert filled with towering rocks. Soon, thousands of climbers from across the country descended on the park. Today "J-Tree" lures tens of thousands of climbers from around the world, and photos of their exploits frequently grace the pages of popular climbing magazines. In the winter, when other world-class destinations like Yosemite are covered in snow, nomadic climbers flock to Joshua Tree in grungy droves.

A comprehensive climbing guide is far beyond the scope of this book, but many great guides are sold in the park's bookstores and in shops outside the park. Among the most popular: Randy Vogel's *Rock Climbing Joshua Tree* and Charlie and Diane Winger's *Trad Guide to Joshua Tree*. Other great climbing resources are the Friends of Joshua Tree, a private, non-profit climbers association formed in 1991 to represent climbers' interests in the park (www.friendsofjosh.org) and the Joshua Tree Climbers' Ranch (www.climbersranch.com)

If you're into rock climbing, check out Nomad Ventures in the town of Joshua Tree. This climbing-centric store offers a huge selection of guidebooks and the region's most extensive selection of climbing gear.

If you want to take climbing lessons, there are a handful of commercial outfitters that offer private guiding, group lessons, and half day climbs. Whether you're a beginner looking to learn the ropes or an advanced climber hoping to sharpen your skills, the following outfitters can get you going: Wilderness Outings (877-494-5368, www.wildernessoutings.com), Uprising Adventure Guides (888-CLIMB-ON, www.uprising.com), and Vertical Adventures (800-514-8785, www.vertical-adventures.com).

Though remarkably safe when done properly, rock climbing is still a dangerous sport. Visitors climb at their own risk in Joshua Tree National Park. In the event of an emergency, call 909-383-5651 or 911. Emergency-only phones are located at the Intersection Rock parking area next to Hidden Valley Campground and at the Ranger Station at Indian Cove.

OTHER ADVENTURES

BIKING

Off-road biking is prohibited in Joshua Tree National Park, but there are still some good rides on established vehicle roads. Park Boulevard, which runs through the Mojave Desert half of the park, offers Joshua Tree's best biking, passing by some of the park's most spectacular scenery. Joshua Tree's other main road, Pinto Basin Road, is more rugged and remote, and the scenery, while nice, is generally less interesting. There are also several four-wheel-drive backcountry roads in the park, but their sometimes sandy composition can make biking difficult.

FOUR-WHEEL-DRIVE ROADS

Joshua Tree has several rugged dirt roads that are best suited to four-wheel-drive vehicles. The most popular 4WD road is the 18-mile round-trip Geology Tour Road (p.149). At the southern tip of the Geology Tour Road is Berdoo Canyon Road (p.158), which heads to the park's southern boundary. Covington Flats (p.173) turns off Highway 62 between Indian Cove and Black Rock Canyon. But if you're really looking for a rugged adventure, check out Old Dale Road or Black Eagle Mine Road (p.203) in the southern half of the park (and be prepared for some nicks and scratches on your pretty SUV). For your own safety and for the protection of the desert ecosystem, always stay on established backcountry roads.

HORSEBACK RIDING

Joshua Tree is a terrific horseback riding destination, with over 200 miles of equestrian trails and trail corridors provided for in the park's Backcountry and Wilderness Management Plan. Both Ryan and Black Rock campgrounds have overnight areas for stock animals, but reservations are required (call 877-444-6777 for Black Rock, 760-367-5545 for Ryan). Permits are also required to camp with stock animals in the backcountry (call 760-367-5545). Don't have your own ride? Contact Joshua Tree Ranch for information on guided trail rides (760-902-7336, www.joshuatreeranch.com).

Joshua Tree
BASICS

GETTING TO JOSHUA TREE

Joshua Tree National Park is located in Southern California about 120 miles east of Los Angeles, 160 miles southwest of Las Vegas, and 12 miles northeast of Palm Springs. Interstate 10 runs along the park's southern boundary, and Highway 62 (aka 29 Palms Highway) runs along the park's northern boundary passing through the towns of Yucca Valley, Joshua Tree, and Twentynine Palms.

There are three main entrances to the park: West Entrance, reached from the town of Joshua Tree off Park Boulevard; North Entrance, reached from Twentynine Palms off Utah Trail; and South Entrance, reached from Cottonwood Springs Road off Interstate 10. Three other destinations in the park— Black Rock, Covington Flats, and Indian Cove—are reached by separate roads off Hwy 62.

GETTING AROUND JOSHUA TREE

Since there's no public transportation in or around Joshua Tree, you'll need a car, a bicycle, or a good pair of hiking boots to explore the park.

ENTRANCE FEES

A seven-day vehicle pass ($15) admits the passengers of one vehicle to the park. A seven-day single entry permit ($5) admits one person to the park when entering on foot, bicycle, motorcycle, or horseback. Frequent visitors can buy an annual pass ($30) or the fantastic Interagency Pass ($80), which provides access to all federal recreation sites (including national parks) for one full year.

VISITOR CENTERS

Joshua Tree National Park has three visitor centers, each located near a major park entrance. The **Joshua Tree Visitor Center** is located in the town of Joshua Tree, one block south of Highway 62 on Park Boulevard. The **Oasis Visitor Center** (p.165) is located in Twentynine Palms at the Oasis of Mara, at the junction of Utah Trail and National Park Drive. **Cottonwood Visitor Center** (p.207) is located at Cottonwood Springs, eight miles north of Interstate 10. Each visitor center includes a ranger-staffed help desk, a bookstore, museum exhibits, clean drinking water, and bathrooms.

WHEN TO VISIT

Joshua Tree is a land of extremes, so timing is everything if you plan on hiking, rock climbing, or camping in the park. Summers are scorching hot, with days routinely topping 100°F and nights rarely dipping below 70°F. Winter brings cool days (60°F), freezing nights, and the occasional snowstorm at high elevations. The best time to visit Joshua Tree is in the early spring (March, April) or late fall (October, November), when daytime temperatures are often gorgeous.

WEATHER

Days in Joshua Tree are typically clear with less than 25 percent humidity. The park receives an average of four inches of rain per year, but that number is only an average—in some years the park gets virtually no rain, in other years several inches can fall in a few hours. Weather in Joshua Tree can be wildly unpredictable, so be prepared for anything. Also note that there's generally a 10°F temperature difference between weather reports for Twentynine Palms and the cool, high valleys in the northwest portion of the park.

One Perfect Day in Joshua Tree

Morning - Explore Hidden Valley (p.126)
Late Morning - Barker Dam Trail (p.133)
Lunch at Crossroads Cafe (p.38)
Afternoon - Ryan Mountain Hike (p.174)
Sunset - Drive to Keys View (p.142)
Dinner at 29 Palms Inn (p.38)

Another Perfect Day in Joshua Tree

Morning - Arch Rock Nature Trail (p.191)
Late Morning - Cholla Cactus Garden (p.196)
Lunch at 29 Palms Inn (p.38)
Afternoon - 49 Palms Oasis Hike (p.180)
Sunset at Eureka Peak (p.173)
Dinner at Pappy & Harriets (p.38)

LODGING

There's no lodging in Joshua Tree National Park, but there are dozens of hotels and motels in the towns just outside the park along Highway 62. Rather than wasting all that paper (when all you need is one hotel room), I've posted all lodging info at www.jameskaiser.com.

CAMPING IN THE PARK

Joshua Tree has nine campgrounds with a total of 490 campsites. Fees range from $10–$15 per night. Most campgrounds are first-come, first-served, but Black Rock and Indian Cove accept reservations from September through May up to six months in advance (877-444-6777, www.recreation.gov). Only Black Rock, Cottonwood, and Indian Cove have running water—you must bring your own water to all other campgrounds. All campsites have fire rings, but you must bring your own wood. See pages 32–35 for campground maps and information.

CAMPING OUTSIDE THE PARK

JOSHUA TREE CLIMBERS' RANCH

This private 18-acre campground, located just outside the park and run by the Joshua Tree Climbers Association, offers camping to members of the JTCA or the American Alpine Club. You must be a member to camp here, but membership is free. (www.climbersranch.com)

JOSHUA TREE LAKE R.V. & CAMPGROUND

This family campground, situated on a small fishing lake, offers hot showers, flush toilets, a laundry room, an RV dump station, off-road access, and a kid's playground. (760-366-1213, www.jtlake.com)

ORGANIZED ACTIVITIES

RANGER PROGRAMS

Free ranger programs and campfire talks are offered throughout the year. Weekly schedules are posted at entrance stations, visitor centers, and on the park's website (www.nps.gov/jotr)

DESERT INSTITUTE

This adult education program, run by the Joshua Tree National Park Association, offers a wide range of terrific outdoor courses in the spring and fall. Topics include geology, archaeology, natural history, map and compass skills, desert survival, art courses, and more. JTNPA members receive a 10% discount. (760-367-5535, www.joshuatree.org/dihome.html)

HAZARDS IN THE PARK

DEHYDRATION AND HYPOTHERMIA

By far the greatest hazards in Joshua Tree are dehydration and hypothermia. Because both are largely self-inflicted, they are also the easiest to avoid—just pack plenty of drinks and warm clothing.

ABANDONED MINES

There are nearly 300 abandoned mines in Joshua Tree, many of which contain open shafts and deep tunnels that drop hundreds of feet. Although some mines have been plugged, many remain open. Use extreme caution near old mines.

RATTLESNAKES & SCORPIONS

Although both rattlesnakes and scorpions are found in the park, visitors rarely encounter them. Rattlesnakes are not aggressive if left undisturbed and they will go out of their way to avoid people. Scorpions are not dangerous unless you are allergic to their venom. Avoid both by watching where you step and never putting your hands in places that you can't see.

FLASH FLOODS

Flash floods are a legitimate danger in the desert anytime it rains. When out and about in Joshua Tree, be sure to avoid canyons and washes whenever it rains or when rain clouds threaten overhead.

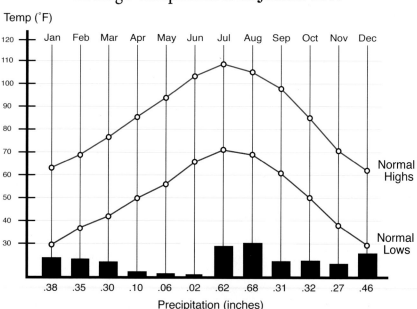

Average Temperatures in Joshua Tree

BLACK ROCK CAMPGROUND

100 Sites
Elevation: 4,000 ft.
Water, Flush Toilets
Fee: $15

HIDDEN VALLEY CAMPGROUND

45 Sites
Elevation: 4,200 ft.
Fee: $10

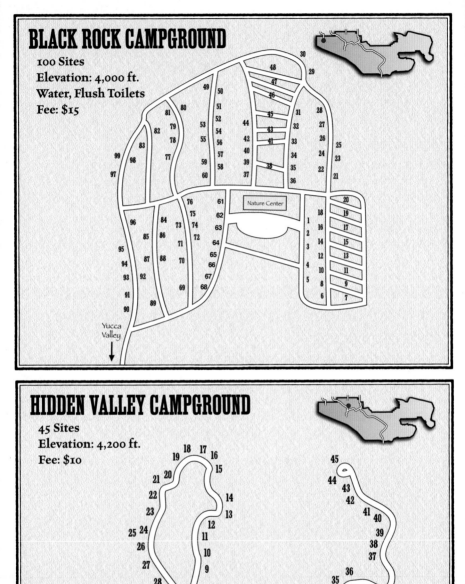

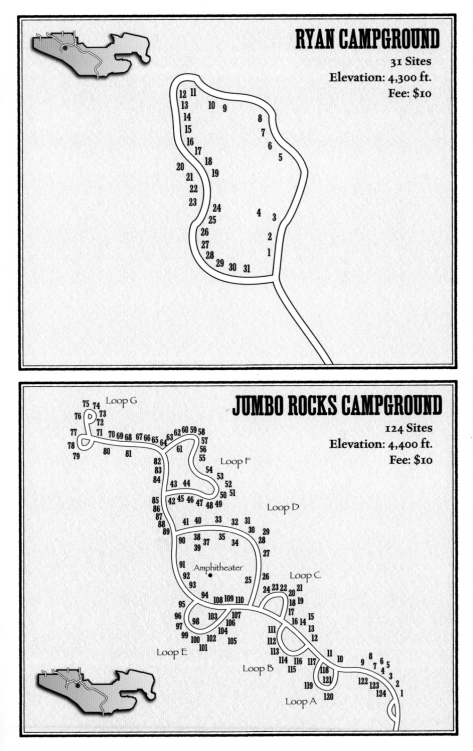

RYAN CAMPGROUND

31 Sites
Elevation: 4,300 ft.
Fee: $10

JUMBO ROCKS CAMPGROUND

124 Sites
Elevation: 4,400 ft.
Fee: $10

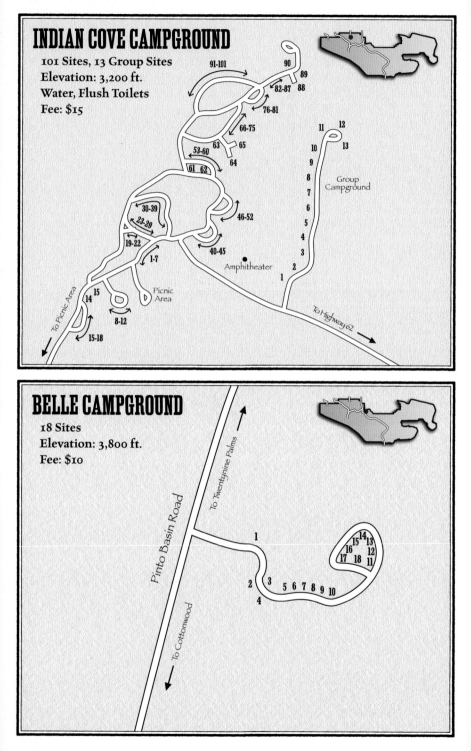

INDIAN COVE CAMPGROUND

101 Sites, 13 Group Sites
Elevation: 3,200 ft.
Water, Flush Toilets
Fee: $15

91-101
90
89
82-87
88
76-81
66-75
63
65
53-60
64
61 62
30-39
23-29
46-52
19-22
1-7
40-45
14 15
Amphitheater
To Picnic Area
8-12
Picnic Area
15-18
To Highway 62

11   12
10   13
9
8
7
6
5
4
3
2
1
Group Campground

BELLE CAMPGROUND

18 Sites
Elevation: 3,800 ft.
Fee: $10

To Twentynine Palms
Pinto Basin Road
To Cottonwood

1
2   3   5 6 7 8 9 10
4
15 14 13
16   12
17 18 11

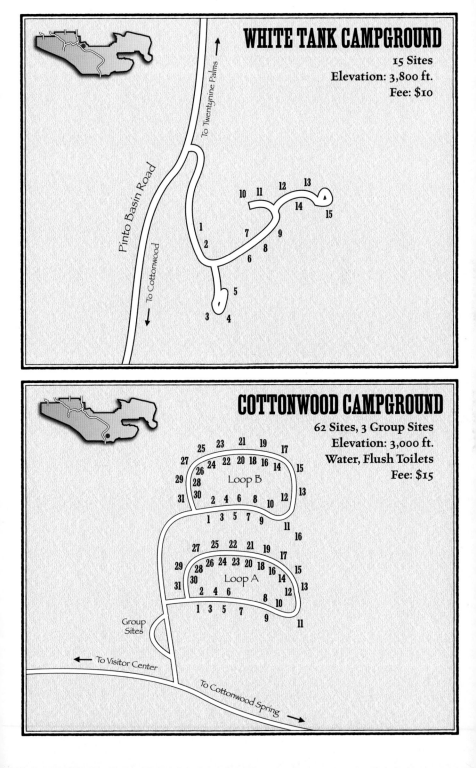

WHITE TANK CAMPGROUND

15 Sites
Elevation: 3,800 ft.
Fee: $10

To Twentynine Palms

Pinto Basin Road

To Cottonwood

COTTONWOOD CAMPGROUND

62 Sites, 3 Group Sites
Elevation: 3,000 ft.
Water, Flush Toilets
Fee: $15

Loop B

Loop A

Group
Sites

To Visitor Center

To Cottonwood Spring

GATEWAY TOWNS

THE TOWNS SURROUNDING Joshua Tree are as varied as the terrain in the park. To the south (in the low, hot Sonoran Desert) lies the densely populated Coachella Valley, home to glitzy Palm Springs and dozens of sprawling, gated golf course communities. To the north (in the high Mojave Desert) are the small, dusty towns of Yucca Valley, Joshua Tree, and Twentynine Palms.

For years the towns just north of the park conjured up images of strip malls, fast food chains, and crew cut Marines. (Twentynine Palms is home to the largest Marine base in the world.) But over the past few years, the tiny town of Joshua Tree—sandwiched between Yucca Valley to the west and Twentynine Palms to the east—has undergone a remarkable transformation. As artists and musicians have discovered the stark scenery and cheap real estate, a scrappy gentrification has taken root. A handful of hip restaurants and art galleries have sprouted up among the creosotes and cacti, luring a steady stream of creative types to the desert. These days Joshua Tree's burgeoning art scene is frequently profiled in major newspapers and magazines.

But long before Joshua Tree became trendy, the High Desert was a magnet for offbeat personalities. In 1941 Edwin J. Dingle, an Englishman who studied meditation and breathing techniques in Tibet in the 1920s, founded the Institute For Mentalphysics—a 420 acre campus in Joshua Tree with buildings designed by Frank Lloyd Wright (www.jtrcc.org). Twelve years later, local resident George Van Tassel supposedly made contact with aliens, and shortly thereafter he built a giant dome called "The Integratron" (p.44).

Today the freewheeling, New Age spirit of the desert is still very much alive. The best way to soak in Joshua Tree's funky personality is to wander among the shops and restaurants near the intersection of and Park Boulevard and Highway 62. There's generally plenty of live music and art gallery showings throughout the week, so ask around. Also check local papers for seasonal attractions such as music festivals and other community events.

Clockwise from Top Left: Crossroads Cafe, Joshua Tree Saloon, used cowboy boots, Sacred Sands B&B

RESTAURANTS

Hidden among postmodern carnage of strip malls and chain restaurants littering 29 Palms Highway (Highway 62) are a handful of terrific, local restaurants. The artsy village of Joshua Tree has the best restaurants, but there are a few gems in Yucca Valley and 29 Palms as well.

★ CROSSROADS CAFE (Brk, Lnch, Din; $6–9, Closed Weds)
Terrific sandwiches, soups, and salads with a funky, laid-back, coffee shop vibe. Over the past decade, Crossroads has become a Joshua Tree institution. The hearty food is the real draw, but they also serve great coffees, smoothies, and beer. (760-366-5414, 61715 29 Palms Highway, Joshua Tree)

★ 29 PALMS INN RESTAURANT (Lnch $7-10, Din $15-22)
Open since 1928, this might be the High Desert's best fine dining. The delicious meals—steaks, seafoods, pastas—are complemented with fresh veggies from their own garden, homemade breads, and a good wine list. (760-367-3505, 73950 Inn Ave, 29 Palms)

★ PAPPY & HARRIET'S (Lnch, Din; $7–18; Closed Tues & Weds)
This old-school honky-tonk serves up tasty cowboy cuisine. In addition to Tex-Mex and burgers ($7–10), they offer terrific BBQ entrées ($17–20). Cold beer is served in mason jars, and the live music is the best around. Reservations are recommended on weekends. (760-365-5956, 53688 Pioneertown Road, Pioneertown)

★ NATURAL SISTERS CAFE (Brk, Lnch; $6–9)
If you like natural, organic, vegan/vegetarian food, this is the place for you. In addition to wraps, soups, and salads they also offer smoothies, fresh juice, baked goods, and free WiFi. This is one of my favorite breakfast spots. (760-366-3600, 61695 Highway 62, Joshua Tree)

★ TEACAKES (Brk, Lnch; $2–3; Closed Tues)
This tiny, French-inspired bakery offers decadent baked goods like muffins, scones, cookies, and danishes. Everything is made fresh from scratch daily, and they also serve terrific coffee drinks. (760-974-6209, 29 Palms Highway, Joshua Tree)

BISTRO 29 (Din; $18–26; Closed Sunday, Monday)
This high-end bistro offers the most upscale atmosphere in the High Desert. Steak, seafood, and Italian classics feature prominently on the menu, and the wine list is one of the most extensive in the region. (760-361-2229, 73527 Highway 62, 29 Palms)

RICOCHET (Brk, Lnch; $5–10)

This tiny restaurant offers an eclectic mix of gourmet goodies: fresh baked muffins, homemade soups, vegan/raw food, and the "Trust the Chef" plate. There's also a terrific selection of cheese, wine, and Belgian ales.
(760-366-1898, 61705 29 Palms Highway, Joshua Tree)

PARK ROCK CAFE (Brk, Lnch; $6–9; Closed Monday)

This quality restaurant offers upscale sandwiches, soups, and salads, plus paninis, quiches, and Italian sodas. They also sell box lunches—perfect for a picnic in the park. Located next to the Joshua Tree Visitor Center in Joshua Tree.
(760-366-3622 , 6554 Park Boulevard, Joshua Tree)

SAM'S PIZZA & INDIAN FOOD (Lnch, Din; $8–12)

Delicious, authentic north Indian food in an unassuming strip mall pizza joint?!? I can't explain it, but I can highly recommend it. Imported Indian beer and imported New Zealand lamb definitely make up for the bland ambiance. They also offer pizza, burgers, and subs.
(760-366-9511, 61380 29 Palms Highway, Joshua Tree)

ROYAL SIAM RESTAURANT (Lnch, Din; $8–12; Closed Tues)

This unassuming restaurant serves classic Thai food at reasonable prices. Although the atmosphere is bland, the food is as spicy as you like on a scale from 1 to 5—and the Chef does not recommend 5!
(760-366-2923, 61599 29 Palms Highway, Joshua Tree)

LA CASITA NUEVA (Lnch, Din; $9–13)

Twentynine Palms Highway is full of mediocre Mexican restaurants, so if you're hankering for Mexican it's easy to end up disappointed. In my opinion, your best bet for Mexican is La Casita Nueva, which features all the classics like tacos, burritos, and enchiladas, plus a great selection of margaritas.
(760-365-5061, 57154 29 Palms Highway, Yucca Valley)

WONDER GARDEN CAFE (Brk, Lnch, Din; $7–10)

This coffee shop/restaurant is your best bet for reasonably priced, healthy, non-fast food in 29 Palms. They serve tasty sandwiches, soups, salads, plus espresso, smoothies. Free WiFi!
(760-367-2429, 73511 29 Palms Highway, 29 Palms)

SANTANA'S MEXICAN FOOD (Brk, Lnch, Din; $3–6)

OK, this cheap take-out Mexican joint will never be considered gourmet during daylight hours. But hey, it's open 24 hours, which means that sometimes the food is divine. Overwhelmed by the extensive menu? Try the Chili Verde burrito.
(760-366-8297, 61761 29 Palms Highway, Joshua Tree)

ENTERTAINMENT

SMITH'S RANCH DRIVE-IN

This drive-in movie theater, open since 1954, is a blast from the past: double feature every night, sound track pumped in through your car's stereo system, all under the twinkling desert stars. Even if both films are less than Oscar-caliber (and I've seen some truly forgettable films here), the old-school drive-in experience is a truly unforgettable experience.
(4584 Adobe Road, 760-367-7713, www.29drive-in.com)

PAPPY & HARRIETS, PIONEER BOWL

Pappy & Harriet's might be the most badass honky-tonk in southern California. In addition to the desert's best live music, it offers great BBQ, pool tables, and a rustic country vibe (760-365-5956). Next door is Pioneer Bowl (760-365-6865), an authentic 1940s-era bowling alley open 2-10 on weekends. Both are located in Pioneertown, north of Yucca Valley. (www.pioneertown.com)

JOSHUA TREE SALOON

This local bar (open every day at 8am) is the most popular watering hole in Joshua Tree. Throughout the week there's live-music, open mic nights, karaoke, and trivia. They also offer burgers and bar food, plus free WiFi.
(760-366-2250, 61835 29 Palms Highway, www.thejoshuatreesaloon.com)

ART GALLERIES

Joshua Tree is home to a thriving arts community, and local gallery openings are the best place to soak in the scene. Check the free local guides (available at stores throughout Joshua Tree) for up-to-date schedules. And don't expect a bunch of snobby hipsters—the Joshua Tree art scene is delightfully mellow and friendly.

OUTFITTERS

NOMAD VENTURES

This is the best outfitter in Joshua Tree, stocked with a huge selection of climbing gear and climbing guidebooks, plus a hearty selection of hiking gear, camping gear, guidebooks, and maps. (760-366-4684, 61795 29 Palms Hwy, Joshua Tree)

COYOTE CORNER

This eclectic store, selling everything from outdoor gear to hippie supplies, is a Joshua Tree institution. Be sure to say Hi to Ethan, the "mayor" of Joshua Tree!
(760-366-9683, 6535 Park Boulevard, Joshua Tree)

JOSHUA TREE OUTFITTERS

This small outfitter offers outdoor gear for sale or rent.
(888-366-1848, 61707 29 Palms Highway, Joshua Tree)

NON-PROFIT ORGANIZATIONS

JOSHUA TREE NATIONAL PARK ASSOCIATION

JTNPA is the official non-profit cooperating association of Joshua Tree National Park. They provide much-needed assistance with park preservation, education, historical and scientific programs. (760-367-5525, www.joshuatree.org)

FRIENDS OF JOSHUA TREE

This rock climbing organization works closely with the National Park Service to preserve the historical tradition of rock climbing in Joshua Tree. (760-366-9699 , www.joshuatree.org)

MOJAVE DESERT LAND TRUST

This conservation minded group works to preserve and protect fragile ecosystems in the Joshua Tree region. (760-366-5440, www.mojavedesertlandtrust.org)

LOCAL FESTIVALS

The funky, fun-loving Joshua Tree community is always looking for an excuse to party, and plenty of great festivals abound. Things kick off in May with the **Joshua Tree Music Festival** (www.joshuatreemusicfestival.com). In September the Joshua Tree Retreat Center plays host to **Bhakti Fest** (www.bhaktifest.com), which features four days of yoga, kirtan, and fire ceremonies. In October, there's the **Joshua Tree Roots Music Festival** (organized by the same people behind the Joshua Tree Music Festival), the **Wild West Coyote Fest**, and **Gram Fest**, a tribute to the late, great country rocker Gram Parsons (p.119).

BEWARE OF
YUCCA MAN!

Every region has its Bigfoot legend, and the deserts around Joshua Tree are no exception. Over the past several decades, there have been scattered reports of a large, hairy, smelly man-beast wandering in and around Joshua Tree National Park. Dubbed "Yucca Man," he is the supposed beastly offspring of human parents who abandoned him in Joshua Tree shortly after his birth. Rather than perish, however, the shaggy infant was adopted by coyotes, and he learned to survive in the harsh desert environment. Today his supposed refuge is the labyrinth Wonderland of Rocks (p.130). But according to one local skeptic: "There are plenty of unshaven, unwashed, overweight men living [here] who fit that description."

· PIONEERTOWN ·

In 1946 a group of Hollywood investors, including Roy Rogers and Gene Autry, built a Western movie set near Joshua Tree called Pioneertown. The outside of Pioneertown looked like a Wild West town, complete with a bank, a jail, a bathhouse, and a saloon. The inside of the buildings, meanwhile, offered modern amenities such as a bowling alley, an ice cream parlor, and a motel for actors and writers. Today the motel rooms are still for rent, the bowling alley is open on weekends, and the former cantina is Pappy & Harriets, a legendary honky tonk famous for great barbecue and live music. To get to Pioneertown, head five miles north on Pioneertown Road off Highway 62 in Yucca Valley (www.pioneertown.com).

THE INTEGRATRON

In 1947 George Van Tassel, an aeronautical engineer who once worked with Howard Hughes, built a small airport in Landers, California, about 10 miles north of Joshua Tree. Six years later (according to Van Tassel) he made contact with aliens who arrived in Landers from Venus. After inviting him onboard their flying saucer, the aliens entrusted him with a technique for rejuvenating living tissue. Shortly thereafter, Van Tassel and his family constructed The Integratron, a giant dome "located on an intersection of powerful geomagnetic lines that, when focused by the unique geometry of the building will concentrate and amplify the energy required for cell rejuvenation." To cover the cost of construction, Van Tassel hosted UFO conventions that drew tens of thousands of UFO devotees in the 1950s, '60s, and '70s. Although Van Tassel died in 1978, the Integratron's acoustically resonant dome continues to lure a steady stream of musicians, meditation groups, and UFO enthusiasts. Guided tours and "Sound Baths"—a unique relaxation experience where a Sound Therapist plays harmonic frequencies on quartz bowls—are available by appointment. (760-364-3126, www.integratron.com)

GEOLOGY

JOSHUA TREE'S JUMBLED geology captivates every visitor who sets foot in the park. The scenery is mythical, hallucinatory, and paranormal all at once. Ragged mountains tower above broad valleys filled with spiky, twisted Joshua trees. Surreal granite rock formations, some resembling giant piles of dripped wax, dot thousands of acres of scrubby landscape. Contorted faces and bizarre animal shapes seem to appear in the cracks of the rocks. Add a couple of melting watches and Salvador Dali would feel right at home in Joshua Tree.

You don't need to know anything about geology to enjoy the scenery here. But take the time to learn about the forces that sculpted the landscape, and you'll look upon the park with a fresh set of eyes. The seemingly fixed scenery will roll into motion. Mountains will wash away like piles of sand. Ice Ages will come and go like snowstorms. And 70-ton boulders will dissolve like sugar cubes as you stare across the park.

The story of Joshua Tree's geology begins nearly two billion years ago, when Earth was about half its present age. As eroded sediments washed off ancient continents into the ocean, thick sediment layers accumulated in the waters offshore. Over time, the bottom layers were compressed and fused into sedimentary rock.

Then, around one billion years ago, Earth's continents collided to form a single supercontinent called Rodinia. As the continents collided and smashed into one another, they crumpled along their edges to form vast mountain chains. Some of the previously formed offshore sedimentary rocks were caught up in these collisions, which generated extreme heat and pressure. Over thousands of years, this heat and pressure metamorphosized the sedimentary rock into an entirely new kind of rock called gneiss (pronounced "nice").

The gneiss that formed in the Rodinian mountains is the oldest rock found in Joshua Tree National Park. Similar types of gneiss are also found in Australia and Antarctica, indicating that a chain of Rodinian mountains once stretched across all three continents when they were fused together. Then, around 800 million years ago—200 million years after the formation of Rodinia—Rodinia broke apart. North America drifted toward the equator, and Joshua Tree's gneiss most likely became part of an offshore continental shelf. For the next 250 million years, the Joshua Tree region lay underwater.

Around 280 million years ago, Earth's continents came together again and formed another supercontinent called Pangaea. The Joshua Tree region lay just off the northwest coast of Pangaea, and additional offshore sediments accumulated on top of it. When Pangaea broke up about 210 million years ago, North America drifted west and collided with a vast tectonic plate called the Pacific Plate, which underlies much of the present-day Pacific Ocean. The collision pushed the Joshua Tree region up above water. It also generated intense heat and pressure that exposed the previously formed gneiss to a new round of metamorphism.

As North America continued to push west, it overrode the eastern edge of the Pacific Plate, which was pushed deep below the surface of the Earth in a process called "subduction." As the eastern Pacific Plate subducted under western North America, it was pushed nearly 400 miles below the surface of the Earth and as far east as Texas. All told, up to 12,000 miles of Pacific Plate may have been pushed under North America

Throughout this process, the eastern edge of the Pacific Plate acted like a giant conveyer belt, carrying vast amounts of ocean water deep underground. The friction of the moving plates and the intense interior heat of the Earth caused the ocean water to boil, helping to melt nearby rocks and sending huge pools of magma rising up under Southern California. When the rising magma reached the previously formed gneiss (which was then buried five to 10 miles underground), it stopped rising and cooled into granite. This granite would ultimately form Joshua Tree's famous rock formations, but it would take one last dramatic act of geology before the rock formations fully took shape.

After the underground granite solidified, millions of cracks appeared in the rocks. Some of these cracks formed when Earth's forces pushed the granite up toward the surface, squeezing the rock from below. Other cracks formed from the compressive weight of the rocks laying above. Still other cracks formed when surface erosion removed large quantities of rocks above, decreasing downward pressure on the buried granite and causing it to expand and crack. Eventually Joshua Tree's granite was riddled with cracks (called "joints" by geologists) at a variety of angles.

Over millions of years, as surface erosion removed layer upon layer of overlying rock, Joshua Tree's crack-riddled granite drew closer and closer to the surface. As it approached the surface, it encountered trickling groundwater, which eroded the granite along its cracks. Granite is composed of feldspar and quartz crystals. When feldspar comes into contact with water, it dissolves into clay. This, in turn, loosens the quartz crystals. This ongoing underground erosion sculpted Joshua Tree's granite along its crisscrossed cracks, rounding out the edges and loosening individual chunks of rock. As the years wore on, additional erosion at the surface revealed these sculpted rock formations, which then settled into the park's famous boulder piles.

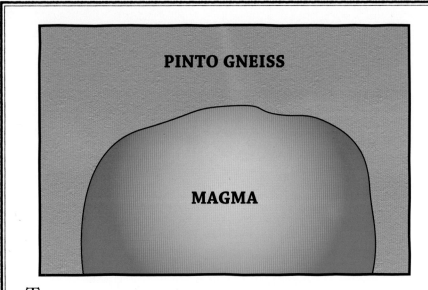

Tens of millions of years ago, giant plumes of magma rose up under Joshua Tree and intruded on a previously formed rock called Pinto Gneiss. At this point both the magma and the Pinto Gneiss were buried several miles underground.

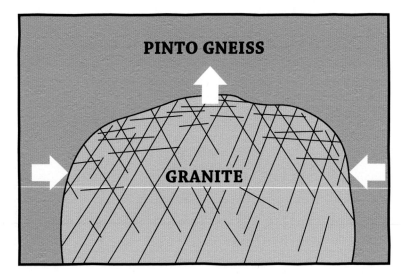

The magma cooled and hardened into granite. As tectonic plates shifted, the granite was exposed to horizontal forces that caused the granite to form diagonal cracks. Meanwhile, as surface erosion slowly removed miles of overlying rock, vertical pressure on the granite was relieved. This caused the previously compressed granite to expand and form horizontal cracks.

Continued erosion of overlying rocks eventually brought the granite close to the surface. The climate of California was much wetter during this time, and as groundwater trickled down, it weathered the granite along its cracks.

As Southern California's climate dried out, less water seeped into the ground and weathering of the granite slowed. At the same time, surface vegetation decreased, slowing the rate of new soil formation and increasing the rate of surface erosion. Eventually, the weathered granite was revealed and loose boulders settled into the strange positions that you see today.

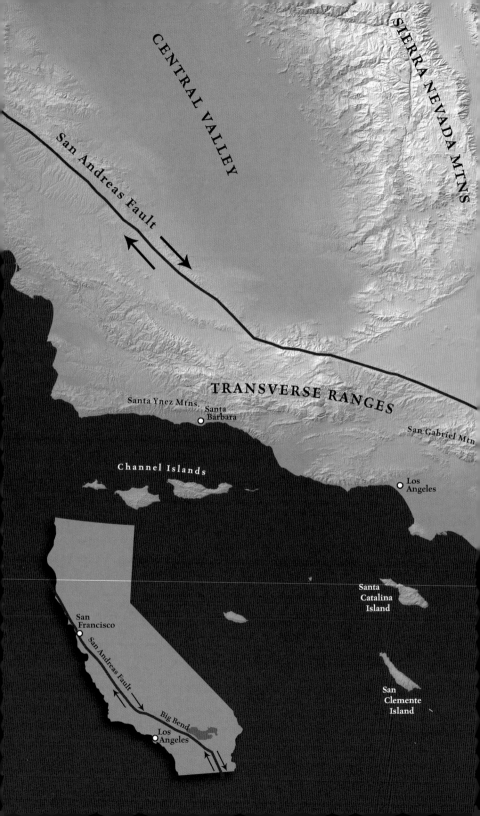

CENTRAL VALLEY

SIERRA NEVADA MTNS

San Andreas Fault

TRANSVERSE RANGES

Santa Ynez Mtns.

Santa
Barbara

San Gabriel Mtn

Channel Islands

Los
Angeles

Santa
Catalina
Island

San
Francisco

San Andreas Fault

San
Clemente
Island

Big Bend

Los
Angeles

Transverse Mountain Ranges

This east-west trending mountain system, stretching from the Eagle Mountains in Joshua Tree to the Pacific Ocean, is a geological oddity in North America, where nearly all mountain ranges trend north-south. The Transverse Ranges were formed by the San Andreas Fault, which stretches hundreds of miles across California and marks the contact zone between two massive tectonic plates: the North American Plate, which is moving south, and the Pacific Plate, which is moving north. These two tectonic plates, which are generally locked in a stationary position, slowly push against each other until they slip, creating earthquakes. The San Andreas Fault runs along California in a relatively straight line, but in Southern California it makes a distinct east-west bend. This bend concentrates pressure in the region, helping to squeeze up mountains in the Transverse Ranges.

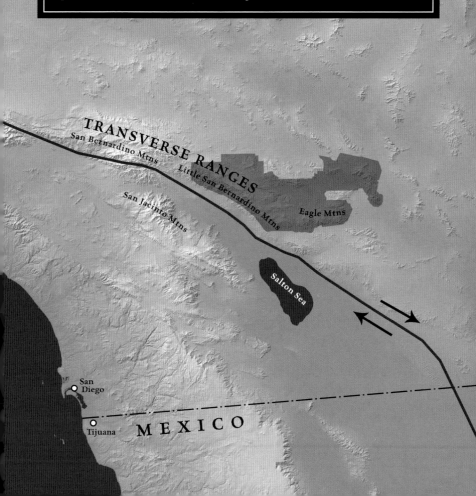

TRANSVERSE RANGES
San Bernardino Mtns
Little San Bernardino Mtns
San Jacinto Mtns
Eagle Mtns
Salton Sea
San Diego
Tijuana
MEXICO

ECOLOGY

STRADDLING THE BOUNDARY between the Mojave and the Sonoran Deserts, Joshua Tree National Park is home to a stunning range of desert plants and animals. Although the barren landscape often seems lifeless, a closer look reveals a thriving ecosystem. Over 50 species of mammals, 40 species of reptiles, and 700 species of plants have been identified in the park. Joshua Tree also lies astride the Pacific Flyway, bringing a wide range of migrating birds through the park. But life in the desert is never easy, and all living things in Joshua Tree must cope with a habitat that is brutal, extreme, and unforgiving.

The defining characteristic of Joshua Tree is its dry, desert landscape, which is influenced by a combination of global and local weather patterns. Southern California lies in a region where the prevailing winds blow in warm, dry air. In Joshua Tree, this aridity is compounded by the local topography. The park is located at the eastern end of the Transverse Mountain Range, which trends east-west across Southern California. Although the land to the west of these mountains is mild and temperate, their eastern slopes descend into some of the most severe desert in North America. In some places mountains covered with pine trees on their western slopes contain only a few desert shrubs on their eastern sides. This dramatic transition is caused by a *rain shadow*, which occurs when mountains wring moisture out of approaching air, creating a dry, desert region on the leeward side. When moist, coastal air travels east across Southern California, it's forced up and over the region's tall mountains. As the air rises it cools, forcing moisture to precipitate out in the form of rain and snow. Robbed of its moisture, the air flows down the mountains' eastern slopes bone dry, creating Southern California's vast desert regions.

But the rain shadow effect is not limited to Southern California. The state's nearly continuous wall of north-south trending mountains is responsible for creating a vast desert region that stretches along much of eastern California. As air flows over these regions, it passes over additional mountains that continue to wring moisture out of the air, helping to extend these deserts across much of the American West. These deserts have been divided up into four major regions: the Mojave, Sonoran, Great Basin, and Chihuahuan Deserts, the boundaries of which are defined primarily by rainfall and elevation.

It's sometimes stated that a desert is any area receiving less than 10 inches of rainfall each year. But this simple definition overlooks the vast complexities of desert ecosystems. Deserts are more accurately defined by a combination of factors, including low rainfall, high temperatures, dramatic temperatures swings, and a high rate of evaporation.

The western half of Joshua Tree National Park marks the southern tip of the Mojave Desert, which generally lies between 2,000 and 5,000 feet in elevation. On average, the Mojave receives three to five inches of rain each year. The Mojave Desert, the smallest of North America's four deserts, covers roughly 50,000 square miles in California, Nevada, and Arizona.

The eastern half of Joshua Tree marks one of the westernmost tips of the Sonoran Desert, which generally lies below 2,000 feet in elevation and experiences searing summer temperatures. The Sonoran Desert covers roughly 86,000 square miles in California, Arizona, and Mexico, including much of the Baja peninsula. (In Southern California, the Sonoran Desert has been further subdivided into a region called the Colorado Desert.)

Joshua Tree is also home to a third ecosystem: the pinyon pine and juniper zone, found at the park's highest elevations. This is the only woodland forest in the park, and it offers abundant shelter, shade, and food resources—pine nuts, juniper berries, acorns—for many animal species. These resources were also extremely important to the survival of early desert people.

Although the rain shadow is the major determinant of the park's climate, several additional factors compound the desert's aridity. Because the air flowing into the desert is so dry, there is very little cloud cover or plant growth, both of which help deflect the sun's rays. As a result, up to 90 percent of solar radiation in the desert reaches the ground. At night, the situation is reversed, and up to 90 percent of the day's accumulated heat is radiated back into the atmosphere through clear, dry skies. (In humid areas, by contrast, only about 40 percent of solar radiation reaches the ground, and the day's accumulated heat is often trapped by clouds at night.) Because deserts gain and lose so much heat over the course of a day, temperature swings are extreme. Daily highs and lows can vary as much as 50 degrees Fahrenheit, and the difference between summertime highs and winter lows can sometimes exceed 100 degrees Fahrenheit.

Although Southern California's mountains block many winter storms that would otherwise reach Joshua Tree from the west, late summer storms sometimes arrive in the park from the south. These storms are often short and violent, sometimes dropping several inches of rain in a few hours and producing deadly flash floods that tear away at the landscape.

Given the extreme nature of Joshua Tree's climate, the plants and animals that live here are truly remarkable. Many are among the most rugged lifeforms in the world. Each species in Joshua Tree has adapted to the harsh environment in its own unique way, but they all share a common talent for surviving on a limited supply of water.

Cold-blooded reptiles are well suited to the desert. Unable to generate body heat on their own, they depend on the environment to regulate their internal temperatures—basking in the sun to keep warm, and retreating to cool hiding places when temperatures soar. Because reptiles burn relatively few calories regulating their body temperature, they require much less food than their warm-blooded counterparts. In the desert, where plant and animal resources are extremely limited, this adaptation is invaluable. Unlike mammals, which spend copious amounts of water cooling themselves through sweating and panting, reptiles have been bodies that are fine-tuned to use a bare minimum of liquid, extracting nearly all the water they need from food. A reptile's dry, scaly skin is another biological adaptation that helps prevent water loss.

Mammals have a much harder time in the desert. Because they must constantly burn calories to regulate their body temperature, they require a steady source of food and water. Due to Joshua Tree's limited resources, overall mammal population densities are very low. Small mammals, which require less food and water, do much better in the desert than large mammals. As a result, nearly half of Joshua Tree's mammals are small rodents. To conserve energy these rodents often spend hot days resting in cool burrows, emerging only a night when temperatures drop. Some rodents avoid summer's scorching temperatures entirely by going into a form of summer hibernation called *estivation*. Large mammals, meanwhile, must always stay close to a constant supply of water. A handful of oases scattered throughout the park provide an invaluable resource for many of the park's larger mammals, most notably bighorn sheep.

Deserts of the World

Roughly one-seventh of the land on Earth is considered desert. One-seventh! That's an area larger than Europe and Australia combined, with Greenland, Madagascar, and Japan thrown in for good measure. Run your finger across a globe along the Tropic of Cancer or Tropic of Capricorn, and you'll find yourself passing over the world's great deserts—the Mojave, Sonoran, Great Basin, Sahara, Gobi, and so on. Viewed from space, these deserts form two distinct, dusty brown bands over the planet. Deserts form for a variety of reasons, but their rough alignment with these two latitudes is more than coincidental.

Most of the sun's energy reaches Earth at the equator, heating the land and water there and creating vast currents of hot, humid air that rise up into the atmosphere. As the air rises, it cools. This forces moisture to precipitate in the form of tropical rainstorms. (These rainstorms are responsible for the tropics—the lush, wet regions on either side of the equator.) Once stripped of its moisture, the dry air falls back to Earth near the Tropic of Cancer and the Tropic of Capricorn. As the dry air approaches the surface of the Earth, it reheats, allowing it to absorb any moisture that might have arrived in these regions on its own. The descending air also creates high pressure zones that divert storms to the north or the south. All of these factors combine to create the two distinct desert bands that stretch across much of the planet.

Bighorn Sheep

Joshua Tree is also home to many insects, spiders, scorpions, and other arthropods. Tarantulas, North America's largest spiders, are most commonly spotted in the fall during mating season. There are also plenty of ants in Joshua Tree, including harvester ants and the unusual honeypot ant, which sometimes swallows so much honey it can no longer move. These gluttonous honeypot ants ultimately become bloated storage jars, providing food for the rest of the colony.

Plants cope with the desert's lack of water in one of three ways: hoarding water for long periods of time; using available water quickly each time it rains before entering long periods of dormancy; or appearing only briefly to produce seeds for the next generation.

Cacti are a good example of the water hoarders, called *succulents*. Their extensive root systems spread out just under the surface of the ground to gather as much water as possible each time it rains. The water is stored in moist, expandable tissues to carry the cacti through long dry spells, and cacti often swell noticeably after periods of rain. Once fully hydrated, succulents can grow for several weeks in dry weather and survive for many additional months. A large barrel cactus can often survive for over a year without rain. But during dry spells these juicy plants often become targets for thirsty desert animals, and many have developed spines, poisons, and other forms of defense to keep such critters at bay.

The second group of plants are the drought tolerators, which lie dormant for much of the year but suck up massive amounts of water each time it rains. Common examples are shrubby plants such as creosotes and brittlebush. These plants often have deep roots that reach all the way down to the water table. (Unlike the shallow root system of succulents, however, such deep roots are poorly suited to sucking up light rains.) When water is plentiful, drought tolerators photosynthesize rapidly, growing as much as possible before the water runs out. When dry conditions return, the plants enter long periods of dormancy. To survive the dry spells, drought tolerators have developed many biological adaptations. Their small leaves require very little water, and they are often covered in a waxy coating to retain moisture. In cases of extreme drought, drought tolerators can shed their leaves entirely to conserve water. Such rugged adaptations allow drought tolerators to survive harsh desert conditions that would kill most other plants.

The third group of plants are the drought avoiders. Desert wildflowers are this group's most famous example. Rather than continuously struggle with the lack of water in the desert, wildflowers wait patiently for optimum conditions before making their appearance. Following adequate winter rains, wildflowers flourish for several weeks in the spring, surviving just long enough to produce seeds for the next generation. Seeds can lie dormant for months or even years before rainfall triggers germination. The seeds of many wildflowers are covered with a resinous coating that acts as a natural auto-timer—only when adequate rains have fallen will the coating be dissolved, allowing the seeds to germinate. This survival mechanism is well suited to desert climates, where rainfall is often sporadic and undependable.

THE JOSHUA TREE

"**G**ROTESQUE." "TORMENTED." "THE most repulsive tree in the vegetable kingdom." To early European explorers, *Yucca brevifolia* was many unflattering things. But to a small band of Mormons passing through the desert in the 1850s, it looked like the prophet Joshua pointing them to the promised land. Although the Mormon's upbeat interpretation was more than a little different from nearly everyone else's, the name stuck, and it has remained the plant's quixotic epithet ever since.

The Joshua tree has fascinated everyone from 19th-century trapper Jedediah Smith to Irish rockers U2, and with good reason. It's the signature plant of the Mojave Desert. In many ways it represents the rugged individualism of the West. Each tree forms a unique profile due to a number of complex environmental factors. But the striking, often garish appearance of the plant is complemented by an equally dynamic private life.

Joshua trees live predominantly in the Mojave Desert, but they can also be found in parts of the Sonoran Desert, Great Basin Desert, and the San Bernardino Mountains. There are two subspecies of Joshua tree: *Yucca brevifolia brevifolia*, which is larger and found in the western Mojave Desert (including Joshua Tree National Park), and *Yucca brevifolia jaegeriana*, which is smaller and found in the eastern Mojave.

Technically, Joshua trees are members of the agave family. And though referred to as trees, their trunks are filled with a fleshy pulp that has no growth rings. As a result, dating Joshua trees is extremely difficult, but specimens reaching heights of 30 feet or more are thought to be several hundred years old. Although Joshua tree sprouts often grow several inches in their first five years, adult trees grow less than one inch per year.

In the spring, blossoms of creamy white flowers sometimes appear on the tips of Joshua tree branches. Blossoming requires a crisp winter freeze followed by adequate spring rain. Researchers believe the winter freeze damages the end of the branch, which stimulates flowering. After a flower appears, the branch splits in two. And after flowers appear on those branches, the branches split again. This random branching accounts for the endless variety of Joshua tree shapes, although some Joshua trees never flower and grow completely straight. As Joshua trees continue to grow, their spiky green leaves die off and fold back, creating the woody shag that covers all but the oldest trees.

One of the most fascinating aspects of the Joshua tree is its relationship with the tiny yucca moth. Joshua trees and yucca moths have evolved to the point where one cannot reproduce without help from the other. When Joshua trees are in bloom, the yucca moth hops from flower to flower and gathers the tree's sticky pollen. The moth then works the pollen into a tiny ball and places it into the stigmatic tube of the Joshua tree, fertilizing the tree. As the moth deposits the pollen, she also lays her eggs. When the eggs hatch, they feed upon the fertilized Joshua tree seeds. Without the moth there would be no seeds, and without the seeds there would be no moths. To ensure a healthy population of Joshua trees, moth larvae only consume about 10 percent of the seeds.

In prehistoric times, the leaves, seeds, and fruits of Joshua trees were a favorite food of the Shasta ground sloth, a giant 500-pound sloth that went extinct near the end of the last Ice Age roughly 13,000 years ago. Prior to its extinction, the sloth's dung inadvertently spread Joshua tree seeds over a vast range. But since the end of the last Ice Age, the Joshua tree's range has shrunk by nearly 90%, which may be partly due to the extinction of the Shasta ground sloth.

In recent years a severe drought has led to the deaths of large numbers of Joshua trees in Joshua Tree National Park. Although the rugged trees can survive for extended periods without rain, during the height of the recent drought thirsty rodents nibbled at the bark of Joshua trees to get at the tree's moist interior. The loss of bark proved deadly for many trees, and hundreds of Joshua trees were lost.

DESERT WILDFLOWERS

WILDFLOWERS ARE TO deserts what fall leaves are to New England. For a few weeks in the spring, given the right conditions, the floor of the desert explodes in color. A kaleidoscope of psychedelic reds, greens, yellows, and blues shimmers in the otherwise sun-baked landscape. There are dozens of wildflower species in the desert, but their delicate and ephemeral nature gives each one an almost dreamlike intensity.

Unfortunately, spectacular wildflower blooms are not an annual event. Many desert wildflowers will appear only following winters with adequate rain. Depending on the amount of rain that falls—or doesn't fall—blooms can be spectacular or nonexistent. This is a biological adaptation on the part of the wildflowers. Given the harsh nature of the desert, wildflowers choose to appear only when conditions are favorable to their survival. Following rainy winters, wildflowers flourish for a few weeks in the spring, produce seeds for the next generation, and then rapidly wilt away in the heat. Their seeds, meanwhile, can lie dormant for several months, or even years, until conditions are once again perfect for the flowers to repeat the cycle.

Over thousands of years, wildflowers have adapted to the desert's notoriously inconsistent weather in remarkable ways. Some species produce seeds covered in a resinous coating that inhibits growth and can only be removed by ample rain. The coating acts as a natural auto-timer, triggering germination only when sufficient water is available. It also protects against events such as scattered showers during a dry spell that would otherwise trick the seed into germinating. When the desert receives torrential winter downpours, often during El Niño years, thousands of wildflowers can bloom in a single location, blanketing the desert in a candy-coated ocean of wildflowers.

Desert wildflowers normally germinate between September and December following periods of adequate rain, but germination does not guarantee a bloom. Only if warm spring temperatures follow adequate winter rains will flower stalks appear and bloom. In Joshua Tree, wildflower blooms often begin in February in the lower, southern portions of the park. Over the following weeks and months, blooms occur at higher and higher elevations, with elevations above 5,000 feet sometimes blooming as late as June.

Blooming Yucca

BARREL CACTUS
Ferocactus cylindraceus

Yellow flowers, 2–3 inches wide, form a crown near the top of the cactus. Barrel cacti can grow up to 10 feet tall in some regions, but they are usually under 5 feet tall in Joshua Tree. The plant's scientific name, *Ferocactus*, is derived from the Latin *ferox*, "fierce."

BEAVERTAIL CACTUS
Opuntia basilaris

Vivid magenta flowers, 2–3 inches wide, appear on the edges of broad, flat stems. Beavertail cacti grow in clusters up to 6 feet wide, and broken-off stems can take root in dry sand. Desert Indians used the fleshy pulp of the cacti to heal wounds.

BRITTLEBUSH
Encelia farinosa

Vibrant yellow flowers, 2–3 inches, on branched stalks. Brittlebush is a silvery, gray shrub, 3–5 feet high, covered with small, hairy leaves. The fragrant stems are burned as incense in churches in Baja, Mexico, where brittlebush is called *incienso*.

CALICO CACTUS
Enchinocereus engelmannii

Pointed magenta flowers surround yellow stamens and green stigmas. The calico cactus (aka hedgehog cactus) grows in clumps of 5–15 small cacti, each supporting a single flower near the top. Generally grows less than 1 foot tall.

CANTERBURY BELLS

Phacelia campanularia

Tiny blue flowers, 1–1.5 inches, fluted with 5 round lobes at the end. Grows up to 2 feet tall. Found on rocky slopes and sandy washes in the southern Mojave Desert. Following wet winters, thousands of canterbury bells can bloom at a single location.

CHIA

Salvia columbariae

Tiny pale blue flowers bloom from a pointy, globular cluster. Stalks, which grow up to 20 inches tall, can have one or two globular clusters. Chia seeds were harvested by desert Indians. The seeds were eaten, brewed to make a thick beverage, and used for medicinal purposes.

CLARET CUP CACTUS

Enchinocereus triglochidiatus

Brilliant red flowers bloom on top of individual cactus heads. Claret cup cactus (aka Mojave mound cactus) grows in clumps up to 3 feet wide and 1 foot tall. Found mostly in pinon/juniper and Joshua tree woodlands above 3,500 feet.

DESERT DANDELION

Malacothrix glabrata

Light yellow flowers with a red spot in the center when young. Often grows in large groups in sandy areas. At night, dandelions close up and hang like drooping bells. The flowers then reopen in the morning. The name "dandelion" is derived from the French *dents de lion* ("lion's teeth").

DESERT MALLOW
Sphaeralcea ambigua

Small shrub with orange, globe-shaped flowers. Stems and leaves are covered with small, star-shaped hairs. Desert Mallow (aka Apricot Mallow) is often found on dry, rocky slopes. The shrub can grow up to 3 feet tall. A perennial favorite among wildflower watchers.

DESERT MARIGOLD
Baileya multiradiata

Yellow flowers with distinct oblong petals. The flower is supported by a narrow stem up to 20 inches long. Desert Marigold generally blooms in the spring, but can also bloom after a late summer rain. The name "Marigold" is derived from "Mary's Gold" in honor of the Virgin Mary.

DESERT WILLOW
Chilopsis linearis

Gorgeous orchid-like flowers grow on this tall tree, which reaches 10–20 feet in height. The 2-inch flowers, whitish pink with well-defined purple lines in the throat, ultimately grow into thin 7-inch fruits. Found in sandy washes below 5,000 feet where water is available for at least part of the year.

DUNE PRIMROSE
Oenothera deltoides

Delicate white flowers, 2–3 inches wide, with petals the consistency of tissue paper. Grows close to the ground in sandy terrain. Releases fragrances at night to attract the white-lined sphinx moth. When the flower dies, its stems curl up and harden into a distinctive globe, often referred to as a "birdcage."

INDIAN PAINTBRUSH
Castilleja angustifolia

Bright red flowers, 1-inch long, bunched at the tip. Often found growing up through other plants, using them for support. Stems grow up to 16 inches tall. Though common throughout the Mojave Desert, its range extends from Southern California to Canada.

MARIPOSA LILY
Calochortus kennedyi

Vivid orange or vermilion flowers, 1–2 inches wide, with 3 large petals. Grows 4–8 inches tall, often in creosote bush scrub or pinon-juniper woodlands. Mariposa lilies were used as food by Indians, who dug up the bulbs and roasted them. *Mariposa* is Spanish for "butterfly"

MOJAVE ASTER
Xylorhiza tortifolio

Purple to pale-blue flowers, 2 inches wide, with a brilliant yellow center. Grows 8–24 inches tall, often on rocky hillsides. Mojave aster (aka desert aster) is very common in Joshua tree woodlands between 3,000–5,500 feet.

NOTCH-LEAVED PHACELIA
Phacelia crenulata

Purple to violet-blue flowers, ½-inch wide, with five round lobes. Leaves are rounded and hairy. Also called scorpionweed because it can cause a skin rash similar to that caused by poison ivy

SAND BLAZING STAR

Mentzelia involucrata

Sand blazing star produces cream-colored flowers that grow up to 2.5 inches long. Its ½-inch fruit contains white seeds that were an important source of food for desert Indians.

SAND VERBENA

Abronia villosa

Tiny pinkish-purple flowers. Grows in small clusters that sometimes carpet vast areas. During the day the vibrant colors attract pollinators. At night the flower releases fragrances to attract moths. Flourishes in sandy areas such as dunes or washes.

SILVER CHOLLA

Cylindropuntia echinocarpa

Greenish-yellow flowers. Grows between 1,000 and 5,000 feet. Named silver cholla because of its brilliant white spines. A member of the cactus family, silver cholla produces a small fruit that is said to smell like rancid butter.

WHITE TIDY-TIPS

Layia glandulosa

White flower, 1–1.5 inches, with crisp petals that radiate around a yellow center. A member of the sunflower family. Grows in open sandy soils below 8,000 feet.

Sacred Datura

Datura wrightii

These dazzling white flowers often appear in the spring, but they can bloom at any time of year given enough rain. Originally a native of Mexico, datura now grows on sandy roadsides throughout the Southwest. Its large, trumpet-shaped flowers emit a foul smell, and they are sometimes streaked with lavender depending on the specific variety. In addition to its striking appearance, datura is famous for the central role it played in the religious ceremonies of desert Indians. Although extremely toxic, the plant contains large doses of hallucinogenic alkaloids that shamans used to induce visions. Datura ceremonies frequently focused on rites of passage such as the transition into adulthood. Visions a young Indian received helped determine his future role within the tribe.

But before you peyote-popping, Merry Prankster wannabes start munching on datura to help you and the Lizard King try to find Great Spirit, keep in mind these typical firsthand accounts plucked from the Internet: "Nothing about this experience was pleasant," "It was such a nightmare," "I will *never* try this again," "I'm still recovering a year later," "Only for those who want to be able to say that they tried EVERYTHING." It's safe to assume that the people who posted these descriptions are generally inclined to view hallucinogenic plants growing abundantly on the side of the road pretty optimistically—and even they hated it. Datura is not fun and it can kill you, so don't eat it.

Creosote Bush

Larrea tridentata

Ranging from California to west Texas and covering nearly a quarter of Mexico, the creosote bush is the most widespread desert plant in North America. It grows up to 10 feet tall and is distinguished by its rounded shape, angular stems, and tiny olive green leaves. Following periods of rain, small yellow flowers and fuzzy white seed-balls appear on the plant. For millions of years, creosotes lived only in the remote deserts of Argentina. Then, roughly 20,000 years ago, the plant suddenly appeared in North America. Some scientists have speculated that a lone creosote seed may have been transported to North America lodged in the feathers of a migrating bird. However it happened, the newly arrived creosote found itself in an ecosystem with no natural predators, and it proceeded to spread like wildfire. Creosote roots can release toxins and choke off the water supply of surrounding plants, creating barren "dead zones" around each creosote. They can also survive in areas where temperatures exceed 120 degrees Fahrenheit and droughts last over a year. When faced with severe drought, creosotes shed their mature leaves and rely solely on newer, smaller leaves that require less moisture. Creosote leaves are also covered with a waxy resin that helps prevent moisture loss and repels animals with its terrible taste. The resin also releases a pungent, slightly medicinal smell when wet, instantly recognizable to the inhabitants of northern Mexico who call the plant *bedionilla*, "Little Stinker."

Creosote Blossoms

Roadrunner
(Geococcyx californianus)

Roadrunners reach up to two feet in length and are found in the American Southwest and northern Mexico. Unable to fly more than a few dozen yards, they are gifted runners that can accelerate fast and reach top speeds of 20 mph. Roadrunners are also highly maneuverable, using their wings and tail as air rudders, allowing them to brake and turn on a dime. Their diet consists primarily of insects and reptiles, but they also eat dangerous animals like rattlesnakes, scorpions, and black widows. Roadrunners are also the only true predator of tarantula hawks.

Cactus Wren
(Campylorhynchus brunneicapillus)

Cactus wrens—North America's largest wrens—grow up to eight inches long and are found throughout the desert Southwest. Both males and females have a brown coloration distinguished by a long, slightly down-curved beak, densely spotted breasts, and a white stripe over the eye. Cactus wrens often build their nests in thorny desert plants, such as cholla or mesquite, which offer good protection from predators. The football-shaped nest also has a side entrance for added protection. Cactus wrens forage on the ground for insects and spiders, and they obtain nearly all of their water from such food.

Gambel's Quail *(Callipepla gambelii)*

Gambel's quail are easily recognized by their top knots—tufts of feathers sprouting dramatically from the top of their heads. Mature birds grow up to 11 inches long, and males are generally more colorful than females. Gambel's quail are good runners that prefer to remain on the ground, but they will take flight to escape predators, cross obstacles, or fly to a roost at night. They are often spotted wandering in groups, called coveys, of up to 16 birds.

Tarantula
(Aphonopelma iodium)

Tarantulas—the largest spiders in the world—measure up to eight inches long from leg to leg in Joshua Tree. Covered with thousands of sensitive hairs that detect the motion of nearby prey, tarantulas will eat anything they can chase down and subdue, including beetles, grasshoppers, lizards, and small mammals. Once captured, prey is injected with a paralyzing venom. A digestive enzyme is then secreted that liquefies the victim's internal organs, which the tarantula sucks out with a straw-like mouth. (Although painful, tarantula bites are harmless to humans.) Tarantulas are best spotted during mating season in the fall, when male tarantulas wander in search of female burrows.

Tarantula Hawk
(Pepsis formosa)

This large wasp, which grows up to two inches in length, is one of the tarantula's most deadly predators. After stinging a tarantula with a paralyzing venom, a female tarantula hawk will drag the spider back to its burrow, lay her eggs on its body, and then seal the burrow—effectively burying the spider alive. When the wasp larvae hatch, they feast on the still-living tarantula, munching on non-essential body parts first to keep the spider alive and maximize freshness.

Giant Hairy Scorpion (Hadrurus hirsutus)

Growing up to five inches long, the giant hairy scorpion is the largest scorpion in the United States. Although common in Joshua Tree, they are nocturnal and rarely seen. Scorpions feed on insects, lizards, and other scorpions, and they are preyed upon on by roadrunners, owls, and coyotes. Scorpions detect prey by sensing minute vibrations on the ground, and their eyes are exceptionally sensitive in low light. Their famous stinger, located at the tip of their tail, is used to stab victims and inject venom. When prey cannot be subdued with pincers alone, the stinger is thrust over the scorpion's head. Although the sting of the giant hairy scorpion is painful to humans, the venom is generally harmless—about the same as a bee sting.

BIGHORN SHEEP

Ovis canadensis nelsoni

The desert bighorn sheep is one of the West's most magnificent and elusive animals. Although bighorns grow up to 250 pounds, they can walk along two-inch ledges and jump down 20-foot inclines with grace. The ram's legendary horns, which take up to a decade to grow, curve up and over the ears in a C-shaped curl. A large pair of horns can weigh up to 30 pounds and reach 30 inches in length. During mating season, competing rams charge each other head on at speeds topping 20 mph. When rams collide, their horns smash together, producing a loud crack that can sometimes be heard for miles. Thickened skulls allow rams to withstand repeated collisions. Rams with the biggest horns generally do the most mating, but if horns start to block peripheral vision they are often "broomed"—deliberately rubbed down on rocks or broken at the tips. There are three herds of bighorns in Joshua Tree, and they are generally spotted in the steep, rocky terrain of the Little San Bernardino Mountains, the Eagle Mountains, and the Wonderland of Rocks. Today roughly 13,000 desert bighorns remain throughout the West, but this is only 10% of their historic, pre-settlement population.

U.S. RANGE

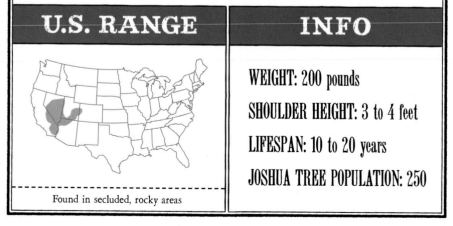

Found in secluded, rocky areas

INFO

WEIGHT: 200 pounds

SHOULDER HEIGHT: 3 to 4 feet

LIFESPAN: 10 to 20 years

JOSHUA TREE POPULATION: 250

COYOTE

Canis latrans

Coyotes are one of the most commonly spotted animals in the park. But even if they prove elusive during the day, you can generally hear their barking yawls at night. Historically confined to the open spaces of the West, coyotes spread rapidly throughout the country following the extermination of wolves in the 1800s. Intelligent animals with a knack for scavenging, coyote populations have held steady and even increased in the East despite years of being hunted, poisoned, and trapped. Coyotes are now found throughout the continental United States and Alaska. Their diet consists mostly of small mammals, but coyotes will eat just about anything, including birds, snakes, insects, and trash. Desert coyotes generally weigh about half as much as other coyotes and have paler, thinner fur that provides better camouflage and helps dissipate heat. Coyotes played a central role in the legends and myths of desert Indians. Among a small cast of human and animal characters, Coyote was portrayed as a scheming, meddling trickster, often scraping by on his cunning and charm. The word "coyote" is derived from the Aztec word *cóyotl*, and coyote's Latin name, *Canis latrans*, means "barking dog."

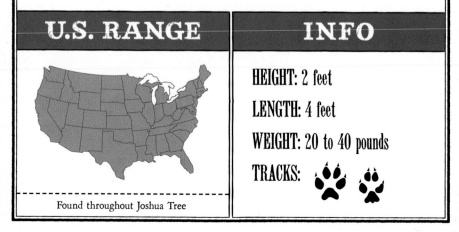

U.S. RANGE

Found throughout Joshua Tree

INFO

HEIGHT: 2 feet

LENGTH: 4 feet

WEIGHT: 20 to 40 pounds

TRACKS:

DESERT TORTOISE

Gopherus agassizii

Desert tortoises, the largest and most magnificent reptiles in Joshua Tree, are slow-moving giants that can live to be 100 years old. Although found throughout the park, they are a rare sight, spending up to 95 percent of their time underground where temperatures are cooler. Their sharp claws are well adapted to digging burrows, which can sometimes reach up to 30 feet in length. Speedy tortoises have been clocked at 0.2 mph. As such, a tortoise will rarely wander more than a few miles from its birthplace over the course of its life. Females lay an average of five eggs, and incubation temperatures determine whether the eggs will develop into males or females. When two adult males encounter each another in the wild, they will sometimes fight and try to flip the other one over. If an overturned tortoise cannot right itself, it will often die of suffocation, sun exposure, or freezing to death. Today these ancient creatures face a variety of modern threats, including habitat loss, exotic disease from pet turtles released in the wild, and speeding vehicles. The desert tortoise is currently listed on both the California and Federal Endangered Species List. If you are lucky enough to encounter a desert tortoise in the park, please do not disturb it.

U.S. RANGE

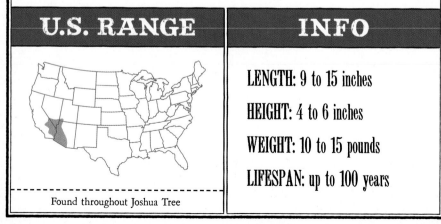

Found throughout Joshua Tree

INFO

LENGTH: 9 to 15 inches

HEIGHT: 4 to 6 inches

WEIGHT: 10 to 15 pounds

LIFESPAN: up to 100 years

JACKRABBIT

Lepus californicus

Jackrabbits are among the park's most commonly seen critters. Found throughout the West, they were originally called "jackass rabbits" because their ears reminded early setters of donkey ears. Jackrabbits have highly advanced senses and reflexes to avoid predators such as coyotes, bobcats, and owls. Their giant ears give them exceptional hearing, and their eyes are pushed so far apart that they have almost full, 360-degree vision. When alarmed, jackrabbits freeze to avoid detection, moving only their ears to catch sounds. If necessary, they can flee at speeds topping 35 mph, making sharp zigzags to confuse predators and hopping up to 20 feet in a single bound. When running at moderate speeds, jackrabbits jump high on every forth or fifth hop to scan their immediate surroundings. Jackrabbits mate and give birth year-round and can produce up to 32 offspring per year. Young jacks hop after their mothers soon after birth. During the day, jackrabbits often rest in the shade of dense vegetation, becoming active only in the late afternoon or at night when temperatures drop. Jackrabbits are strict vegetarians.

U.S. RANGE

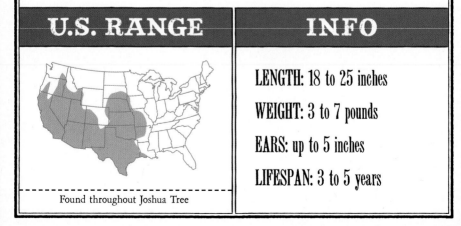

Found throughout Joshua Tree

INFO

LENGTH: 18 to 25 inches

WEIGHT: 3 to 7 pounds

EARS: up to 5 inches

LIFESPAN: 3 to 5 years

RATTLESNAKES

Crotalus scutulatus scutulatus (below), Crotalus atrox (right)

Rattlesnakes are considered some of the most highly evolved snakes in the world, capable of capturing, killing, and ingesting relatively large prey. Their namesake rattle consists of a series of dry, interlocking segments that produce a distinct rattling noise when shaken. It is used as a warning device when the rattler is threatened. A new segment is added to the rattle each time the snake sheds its skin—about two to four times per year. Although rattlesnakes have poor eyesight, they have a sharp sense of smell and can detect body heat through infrared sensors located on either side of their head. These keen senses are used to detect prey such as rodents and small birds while a rattler lies in wait. When the rattler strikes its victim, it injects a paralyzing venom through sharp fangs. Once the victim is motionless, the rattler swallows it whole. Rattlers, in turn, are preyed upon by coyotes and hawks. Hawks will pluck a rattler from the ground and drop it repeatedly from the air until the snake is dead. The Mojave Rattlesnake (above) has one of the most toxic venoms of any North American rattlesnake. The Western Diamondback (right) is the largest rattlesnake in the West, growing up to seven feet long.

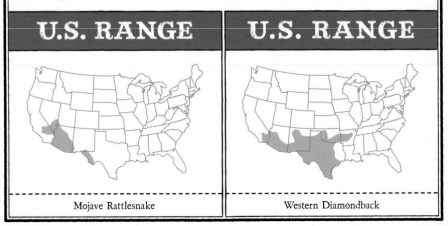

U.S. RANGE

Mojave Rattlesnake

U.S. RANGE

Western Diamondback

CHUCKWALLA

Sauromalus ater obesus

This potbellied reptile, a member of the iguana family, is the largest lizard in Joshua Tree National Park and the second largest lizard in North America (after gila monsters). Western chuckwallas are characterized by thick tails and loose folds of skin around the neck and shoulders. In the morning, they bask in the sun until their body temperature reaches 100°F, at which point they begin searching for food. Strict vegetarians, chuckwallas browse on leaves, buds, flowers, and fruit. They are said to be particularly fond of yellow flowers such as brittlebush. When frightened, chuckwallas retreat to rocky crevices and wedge themselves in place by inflating their lungs up to three times normal breathing capacity. Desert Indians, who hunted chuckwallas for food, would puncture the inflated lizard with a sharp stick to remove it from its hiding place. Chuckwallas mate in the spring, and females lay clutches of five to ten eggs in the summer. When resources are abundant, a single large male will sometimes dominate his local territory. Chuckwallas defend their territory through physical displays that include push-ups, head-bobbing, and gaping of the mouth.

U.S. RANGE

Found among large rocks and boulders

INFO

LENGTH: 11 to 16 inches

WEIGHT: up to 2 pounds

LIFESPAN: 25 years

There were only so many ways to scrape out a living in the desert, however, and in terms of day-to-day activities the Serrano and Cahuilla were virtually identical. The same was true of most desert tribes in Southern California, where the harsh environment forced them to adapt in remarkably similar ways. The limited resources kept population densities low. Villages generally consisting of 25 to 100 individuals—a stark contrast to Indians living on the coast where natural resources were abundant and village populations sometimes topped 1,000.

Desert Indians were hunters and gatherers, but up to three-quarters of their diet consisted of plants. Although acorns, mesquite beans, and pine nuts were their most important sources of food, they ate over 100 different varieties of plants. Because different plants have different growing seasons, desert Indians were highly mobile, moving from one harvesting site to another throughout the year.

Desert Indians generally avoided hunting large animals like bobcats and bighorn sheep. Instead they focused their energy on smaller animals such as jackrabbits and rodents, which were more plentiful, less dangerous, and much easier to hunt. Their weapons included bows, arrows, and throwing sticks similar to boomerangs that were used to break animals' legs. Rodents that hid in rock crevices or holes were extracted with long, forked sticks that were twisted into the animal's fur. But desert Indians were not particularly picky eaters, and their diet also included snakes, lizards, and insect larvae. Crickets were sometimes roasted as a condiment for acorn mush. Despite their appetite for just about anything that moved, they were also known to keep animals such as dogs, birds, and reptiles as pets.

In the winter, desert Indians wore clothing made of animal skins. In the summer they wore few clothes at all. Indian women were highly skilled weavers, and they spent much of their time weaving plant fibers from yuccas and palm

Serrano & Cahuilla pottery & basketry

trees into hats, sandals, and practical items such as baskets, netting, and rope. A women's social prestige within the tribe was often based on her weaving ability. Pottery was also common among desert Indians, and earthenware vessels called *ollas* were used to store water and food.

Serrano and Cahuilla Indians lived in thatched huts made from palm fronds. Each family lived in a circular house with a central fire pit, but most daily routines took place outside. During the day, Indians often sat in the shade of a *ramada*, a thatched canopy supported by four poles. Villages also had several communal structures such as buildings for storage, a sauna-like sweat house, and a large ceremonial room where the village leader lived.

Although each village had a leader, daily life revolved around the family. Family members depended on one another for survival, and the close bonds they developed lay at the heart of Indian society. The importance of family was reflected in their vocabulary—the Cahuilla had over 60 words to describe relatives and relationships.

Both the Serrano and the Cahuilla split their tribe into two distinct groups called *moieties*, based on male family lineage. The two moieties—*Tukum* ("Wildcats") and *Wahilyam* ("Coyotes")—served mostly as marriage guides; a Wildcat could marry a Coyote, but not another Wildcat (and vice versa). These rules ensured a healthy and diverse gene pool. It also forced Indians to seek partners outside of their local village, strengthening overall alliances within the tribe.

EUROPEAN COLONIZATION

BY MOST ACCOUNTS the Serrano and Cahuilla led happy, comfortable lives. Although natural resources were limited in the desert, the Indians made the most of them, and both tribes generally enjoyed peaceful relations with their neighbors. The combined population of the Serrano and Cahuilla tribes probably never exceeded more than 3,000 individuals, but each tribe contributed to California's unique native culture.

By the time Columbus set sail there were roughly 100,000 Indians living in California, representing about 60 or so individual tribes. When Spain defeated the Aztecs in Mexico in 1521, all of Mexico fell under its control. Two decades later, Juan Rodriguez Cabrillo sailed north from Mexico to explore the coast of California. Although Cabrillo recorded favorable impressions of the land, Spain saw little in the way of economic opportunity. California lay a half world away from European centers of trade, and for the next two centuries California served mostly as a backdrop for smugglers sailing between Mexico and the Orient. But when Russian fur trappers began venturing down the California coast in the mid-1700s, Madrid immediately took notice. To "guard the dominions from all invasion and insult," Spanish officials ordered the construction of 21 missions along the California coast—a turn of events that would have a profound impact on the Serrano and Cahuilla tribes.

In 1771 Mission San Gabriel Archangel was constructed in present-day Los Angeles. This marked the first European presence anywhere near Serrano and Cahuilla territory, but the two tribes were only indirectly affected. Although Spanish goods sometimes drifted into the desert along Indian trade networks, there was little contact with European settlers. In 1772 Pedro Fages, a Spanish military officer, became the first European to enter the Mojave Desert when he went looking for military deserters. But Fages' journey was brief and of little consequence.

Four years later, a Franciscan missionary named Francisco Garcés undertook the first meaningful European exploration of California's deserts—a 2,000-mile trek that lasted 11 months. Garcés "went native," adopting the clothes and eating habits of the desert tribes and chronicling their behavior in his journal. Among other things, he noted a thriving Indian slave trade carried out by the Mohave Indians, the largest and most powerful tribe he encountered.

For the most part, however, the Spanish avoided the deserts. They were far more focused on their growing problems along the coast. Uprisings among Mission Indians were becoming common. Those Indians who managed to escape the mission often fled to the remote deserts and mountains to the east. While there, they recruited local Indians to perform raids on Mission flocks. To bring these more remote tribes under control, the Spaniards built a second, interior chain of Mission outposts called *asistencias* that ran parallel to those on the coast.

Spanish Mission

In 1819 Mission San Gabriel built an asistencia in Redlands, less than 40 miles from present-day Joshua Tree National Park. Serrano and Cahuilla Indians living near Redlands were soon under Spanish control, but more distant villages, such as the Oasis of Mara, were still sheltered by the rugged Little San Bernardino Mountains.

Just two years after the asistencia in Redlands was established, the Mexican Revolution ended Spanish control of California. Within a few years the Mission system dissolved. The Indian transition into Mission life had been a difficult one, but the transition out proved just as taxing. Many former Mission Indians were hired as cheap labor by the powerful Mexican ranchers who now controlled the region. But the ranchers stayed clear of the deserts, allowing the Indians who lived there to carry on their traditional lifestyle.

A few decades later, explorers from the east began arriving in California. Most were destined for the coast, but several passed through Serrano and Cahuilla territory along the way. Fur trapper Jedediah Smith crossed the Mojave Desert north of Joshua Tree in 1826, and Kit Carson followed in his footsteps a few years later. When explorer John Fremont passed through the Mojave in 1844, he noted: "From all that I heard and saw I should say that humanity here appears in its lowest form and in its most elemental state." He then went on to describe the Joshua Tree as "the most repulsive tree in the vegetable kingdom."

Fremont's gruff description was typical of white attitudes towards deserts at the time. In the days before air conditioning and automobiles, deserts were considered deadly, hostile terrain—a stereotype that was well justified. The first Spanish expedition into the desert was only organized after a group of military deserters fled there hoping they wouldn't be followed, and only a handful of expeditions were organized after that. By the time the United States gained control of California in 1848, its deserts were among the most remote and unexplored regions in the country. But all that was about to change.

SMALLPOX INVADES THE DESERT

ON JANUARY 24, 1848, nine days before Mexico officially handed California over to the United States, gold was discovered in Northern California. Although both countries were unaware of this fact when the papers were signed, within a few months the biggest gold rush in the history of the world was on. Prior to the discovery of gold, there were only a few thousand white settlers living in California. In 1849 alone, over 80,000 people flooded the state. Ten years later, California's population was nearing 400,000.

California was booming, but the tidal wave of humanity was concentrated almost entirely in the northern half of the state. In 1860, over a full decade after the Gold Rush kicked off, Los Angeles was still a small cattle ranching town with

Acorns & Indians

Of all the world's early human cultures, only in North America did complex inland societies evolve in the absence of agriculture. All other complex societies, from the Egyptians to the Aztecs, fueled their development on irrigated crops, which are highly nutritious and capable of mass production. But Indians north of Mexico were not only able to survive without large-scale farming, they advanced to the point of developing complex, multi-tiered societies run by ruling elites and distinguished by ritual specialists and skilled craftsmen. Anthropologists had once assumed that agriculture was essential for such a feat. The Indians of North America proved them wrong.

What made the Indian's situation different was North America's staggering abundance of natural resources. Even away from the lush, coastal regions, the continent's unique topography lent itself to a wilderness flush with wild game and edible plants. Although both were eaten, plants were the most important food source. And from the deserts of California to the forests of New England, the most important plants were oak trees for the acorns they provided.

In other parts of the world, nuts are covered in shells so thick you need a hammer to open them (think macadamias and brazils). But North American varieties are different. Here, nuts like acorns are thin-shelled and easy to open. They are also highly nutritious and can be harvested in huge quantities. At large oak groves, a single adult can collect several tons of acorns over the course of a two-week harvest. Acorns can also be stored for up to a year without spoiling because of the presence of a natural preservative called tannin. Tannin increases the acorn's shelf-life, but it also makes them bitter and unpalatable (it's the same chemical used to tan leather). To make the acorns edible, Indians would grind them into an oily meal which was then filtered repeatedly with water to leach out the tannin. The resulting flour was then cooked into a gruel-like soup or tortilla-style flatbread.

The autumn acorn harvest was such an important event to the Indians of Southern California that elaborate rituals and ceremonies developed around it. When the acorns finally ripened in the fall, village leaders would proclaim a three-day festival of feasting, singing, and dancing to celebrate the new crop.

a little over 2,000 full-time residents. The deserts to the east were even more untouched. In 1853 a scout for the U.S. Railroad Survey wrote of the region surrounding Joshua Tree: "Nothing is known of this country. I have never heard of a white man who had penetrated it."

Since the arrival of the Spanish, California's deserts had acted as a kind of natural barrier between the Indians that lived there and the settlers clustered along the coast. During the first decade of the Gold Rush, when Indian populations across much of the state were decimated, tribes living in the remote deserts remained relatively unaffected. But in 1863 this natural barrier was shattered when a smallpox epidemic swept through Los Angeles and headed east. Within a matter of weeks, many Serrano and Cahuilla had fallen ill.

For centuries desert shaman had treated sick Indians by sending them into sweat houses (enclosed shacks heated by a small fire) where sick Indians sweated profusely for hours. This treatment was believed to cleanse the body and promote health. But the results were disastrous when applied to smallpox. Sweating rapidly increased the rate of transmission, and soon the virus had blanketed the desert. Indian populations plummeted, and whole villages were abandoned. Within a matter of months, the social and political structures that had governed desert Indians for centuries started to fall apart.

The Serrano at the Oasis of Mara were among those who abandoned their village. When the survivors returned a few years later, they found a group of Chemeheuvi Indians living among the palms. The Chemeheuvi (sometimes called the Southern Paiute) were the eastern neighbors of the Serrano, but a series of wars with the more powerful Mohave Indians along the Colorado River had driven them west.

Both tribes had fallen on hard times, and they agreed to peacefully share the resources at the oasis. But the Chemeheuvi and Serrano were both facing the end of traditional Indian life. As new settlers continued to arrive in California, Indian populations continued to decline. By the late 1800s over 75 percent of California's Indians had died due to disease and warfare. A government report issued near the end of the century summed up California's Indian situation in one tidy sentence: "Never before in history has a people been swept away with such terrible swiftness."

Smallpox was one of the deadliest killers the world has ever known. The virus wiped out much of the native population in North America, and it killed an estimated 60 million people in Europe in the 18th century alone. In the 20th century smallpox killed an estimated 300–500 million people worldwide. In 1979, after decades of successful vaccination campaigns, the World Health Organization certified the worldwide eradication of smallpox.

GOLD MINERS IN JOSHUA TREE

SMALLPOX CRITICALLY WEAKENED the Indians at the Oasis of Mara, but the final blow came from the rapid development of Southern California in the late 1800s. By the 1850s, ranchers from San Bernardino were driving their cattle into the Mojave Desert, and soon they were venturing into the protected valleys and grasslands in the northern half of Joshua Tree National Park.

Ranching in the desert required about 17 acres per adult animal. But ranchers were often on the go, moving seasonally in search of adequate food and water. As one early rancher put it, "In those days, if you were a cowpuncher, you had a pair of chaps, a horse and a pack horse, a bedroll, salt, staples, a six-shooter, and a big chew of tobacco." The ranchers were the first white men to become familiar with the area, and they built a network of primitive access roads. Many roads were simply improved Indian trails, but their impact on the region was dramatic.

By the mid-1850s the gold fields in Northern California had started to dwindle, and thousands of prospectors fanned out across the state in search of the next big strike. A handful of these prospectors wandered along the roads that led into Joshua Tree, and in 1863 gold was discovered near the Oasis of Mara.

Suddenly, the Indians living at the oasis found themselves sharing its resources with a handful of prospectors. At first the prospectors stayed briefly, but in 1879 the region received its first permanent white settler: Bill McHaney. Just 20 years old, McHaney wound up staying in the area until his death nearly 60 years later. Naturally friendly, he got along so well with the Indians that they showed him the locations of nearby trails, water holes, and deposits of gold.

But the region's defining moment came in 1883, when a prospector named Lew Curtis wandered into the foothills 15 miles east of the Oasis of Mara and discovered deposits so rich that the ground was literally speckled with gold. When the news leaked out, hundreds of prospectors flocked to the area and a boomtown named Dale rose up nearby.

At its rough and tumble peak, Dale was home to over 1,000 citizens—almost one-tenth the size of Los Angeles at the time. Most of Dale's citizens lived in mobile tent structures that could easily be moved to be closer to new strikes. In its early years, Dale's location shifted several times. When the town finally settled down, it included a general store, post office, blacksmith, and saloon. A small shack on a hill overlooking Dale constituted the red light district, jokingly referred to as the "Mayor's Residence."

Dale's first residents collected placer gold—small bits of gold eroded from rich veins and scattered along the surface. When the placer gold was gone, the prospectors turned their attention to the lode deposits buried deep in the surrounding hills. But lode mining was extremely expensive, and as this point well-capitalized mining companies arrived in Dale. Before long, many of the town's citizens were salaried employees.

After working all day in the mines, Dale's residents would descend on the town center in the early evening to gamble and drink into the night. Because there were only a handful of buildings in town, most activities took place outside at tables illuminated by kerosene lanterns. Dale's saloon was reserved for the town's most important citizens, a group that included mine owners, engineers, assayers, and shift foremen. The saloon boasted a primitive air-conditioning system that consisted of a wall of canvas that was kept constantly wet. As water evaporated off the canvas, the inside of the saloon was cooled.

But creature comforts were few and far between in Dale, especially for the working class. Miners worked long physical hours, often in triple-digit heat, and those prospectors who weren't employed by the mining companies often came home empty-handed. Water, pumped in from a well north of town, arrived in Dale tinted brown with minerals and salts. Such living conditions were more than most people could bear. After a few years, the town's population dropped dramatically. Prospectors that did stay continued to scour the region for gold, and occasionally they found it. By the turn of the century, a handful of mines had been discovered within Joshua Tree National Park that rivaled those at Dale, most notably Lost Horse and Desert Queen Mines. For the next several decades, mining operations flourished in Joshua Tree.

Gold Mining

IN THE
Desert

Millions of years ago, gold-bearing magma welled up below Joshua Tree and seeped into cracks in the bedrock. After cooling and hardening, the magma formed long quartz veins speckled with gold particles. Over time, erosion exposed the quartz veins, and small grains of "placer" gold spread out across the landscape. (*Placer* is Spanish for "pleasure"—a reference to the relative ease of gathering this form of gold.) When prospectors first arrived in Joshua Tree in the late 1800s, they collected the small grains of placer gold by dry washing. This involved gathering gold-rich soil in a pan and repeatedly tossing the soil in the air, letting the wind blow away the lighter soil particles and leaving the heavier gold particles behind. Although dry washing was time consuming, it was an easy and inexpensive way to collect gold. Once the placer gold was gone, prospectors turned to the "lode" gold found in the underground quartz veins. They mined massive quantities of quartz ore, which was processed by stamp mills to separate the gold particles from the rest of the rock. Miners were lucky to extract ¼ ounce of gold from one ton of crushed ore.

Stamp Mill

1   Small chunks of crushed ore are placed in a mesh chamber

2   A heavy iron cylinder, the "stamp," moves up and down, pulverizing the ore into a fine rock powder.

3   The rock powder is flushed out with water, spreading rock pulp over the amalgam board.

4   Gold particles chemically cling to mercury on the amalgam board while other particles are washed away. The gold and mercury mixture is then scraped and heated until the mercury vaporizes, leaving gold behind.

Willie Boy

THE WILLIE BOY MANHUNT

I N THE LATE 1800s, the dirt roads that led many white settlers into the region around Joshua Tree were also leading many Indians out. Around this time, Indians at the Oasis of Mara had started accepting seasonal employment at ranches in nearby towns. For a few months each year, families would live at a ranch and collect a steady paycheck. Although Indians were adapting to the modern world, they were also competing directly with poor whites for jobs, and racial tensions flared. Unsolved crimes were often blamed on innocent Indians. Raids sometimes took place in which Indians were brutally hunted down. Near the end of the century, one government employee bluntly concluded that, "Race prejudice is too strong in Southern California to secure a fair administration of justice."

Discrimination from whites was a fact of life in the region, but Indians were also facing problems from within their own tribes. Poverty, alcoholism, and a new generation of young Indians fascinated by white culture were all taking their toll on traditional Indian life. As tribal elders passed away, there were fewer and fewer young Indians left to replace them. Those that could were sometimes reluctant to do so. This inter-generational tension soon came to a breaking point when two young Indians living at the Oasis of Mara fell deeply in love.

In 1909 a 27-year-old Chemeheuvi named Willie Boy became romantically involved with Carlota Boniface, the 16-year-old daughter of one of the leading elders of the Chemeheuvi tribe. When Willie Boy approached Carlota's father, Old Mike Boniface, for permission to marry, Willie Boy was vehemently denied. Both Willie Boy and Carlota belonged to the same tribal moiety, and traditional Indian culture forbid them from marrying. Old Mike was furious that Willie Boy would even consider such a proposition.

Shortly after Old Mike Boniface's denial, Willie Boy and Carlota ran away into the desert. Within a few hours, Old Mike had tracked the couple down and confronted Willie Boy at gunpoint. The young Indians were brought back to the village and physically separated.

A few months later, Willie Boy shot Old Mike Boniface at point blank range and fled into the desert with Carlota at his side. A white posse from the nearby town of Banning was organized to capture the pair. But by the time the posse left, the couple already had a six-hour head start.

The posse returned to Banning three days later with the body of Carlota Boniface. As a horrified crowd gathered, the men explained that she had been shot by Willie Boy when she slowed his escape. According to the posse, he had left her for dead and continued running on his own.

Carlota's murder marked a pivotal turning point in the Willie Boy saga. Prior to her death, many whites had brushed off Old Mike's murder as an Indian dispute that did not concern them. There was even something secretly thrilling about two young Indians running away in the name of love. Carlota's murder changed all that. Suddenly, Willie Boy was no longer a misguided lover but a cold-blooded killer motivated by raw savagery. For decades white settlers had been fighting to civilize the West. Willie Boy's actions represented an affront to their accomplishments. On a much darker level, it also confirmed the suspicions of many settlers regarding the "true" nature of Indian behavior.

Within 24 hours of the first posse's return, reward posters were printed and a second posse was dispatched. As interest in the manhunt grew, local newspapers battled to scoop one another. Their coverage soon degenerated into tabloid fiction playing up popular Western stereotypes. Willie Boy was described as a "redskinned lady killer" as "fickle as he was gallant in affairs of the heart." When one of the posse members claimed, with no evidence, that an empty bottle of whiskey had been found in Willie Boy's bedroom, a paper reported that Willie Boy had consumed, "a suitcase full of whiskey" before shooting Mike Boniface. Before long, a half dozen other gratuitous killings had been added to his record.

For the next several days, Willie Boy used a combination of cunning and speed to elude the posse. He headed east toward Nevada before cutting back to the San Bernardino Mountains, just west of Joshua Tree. As the posse approached the mountains, Willie Boy's tracks started to include a narrow line in the sand. He was dragging his rifle. They were finally wearing him down.

Willie Boy's tracks led to Ruby Mountain, located on the western fringe of the San Bernardinos, and as the posse approached the mountain Willie Boy fired at them from above. One man was seriously wounded. The rest fired back and sought cover. Words and shots were exchanged throughout the day, but the wounded man's serious condition forced the posse to withdraw. Just before the

─── DESERT RUNNERS ───

Willie Boy's physical accomplishments during the manhunt cannot be overstated. For over a full week, traveling on foot, he eluded five men chasing him on horseback, covering nearly 600 miles of harsh desert terrain and sometimes averaging 50 miles *a day*. At times, the posse's horses grew so tired that the men were forced to dismount and continue on foot. Some scholars have suggested that Willie Boy was genetically predisposed to excel at running. For hundreds of years a cult of runners existed within the Chemeheuvi tribe who served as desert messengers, covering vast stretches of unfriendly terrain with astonishing speed. Willie Boy was a gifted baseball player who was known for his athleticism, and it is possible that he was a descendant of the Chemeheuvi's legendary runners.

TELL THEM
WILLIE BOY IS HERE

Exactly 60 years after the Willie Boy manhunt, Universal Pictures released *Tell Them Willie Boy Is Here*, a film loosely based on the actual events. It starred Robert Redford as a fictional sheriff named Cooper, Robert Blake (in redface) as Willie Boy, and Katherine Ross as Willie Boy's lover. The writer and director, Abraham Polanksy, presented a sympathetic, if somewhat awkward story in which Willie Boy ultimately finds himself the victim of conflicting white and Indian cultures.

Around the time of the film's release, some Hollywood luminaries were championing a "new Indian movie" in which traditional western stereotypes were cast aside. Marlon Brando protested Hollywood's depiction of Indians by sending a woman in full Indian headgear to the Oscars in 1973 to accept his Best Actor award for *The Godfather*. The woman, who called herself Sacheen Littlefeet, accepted Brando's award and gave a politically charged speech expressing her views on the depiction of Indians in Hollywood. A few moments later, Clint Eastwood took the stage to announce Best Picture. He prefaced his remarks by saying, "I hope I don't have to present this award to all the cowboys shot in John Ford Westerns."

Jim & Matilda Pine

posse left, a final shot echoed from the mountain. No bullet landed anywhere near the men.

Within hours, news of the shootout reached Banning, and newspapers went to press with heavily fictionalized accounts of the event. While Banning newspapers dished out sensationalized Willie Boy gossip, the town of Riverside, located near Banning, was preparing for the arrival of President William Taft, who was in the middle of a cross-country speaking tour. Taft was followed by an entourage of East Coast reporters. When the reporters learned of the manhunt, they jumped on the story. New York editorial pages were soon fretting that Willie Boy represented a credible threat to the President's life, and newspapers across the country began covering the manhunt.

As outrageous Willie Boy rumors swirled around the nation, a third posse was approaching Ruby Mountain. As they neared the spot where Willie Boy had last been seen, they found his body lying on the ground. It was bloated and sunburned. A rifle lay by his side. At the end of the shootout with the second posse, Willie Boy had removed his shoe, pointed his rifle at his chest, and pulled the trigger with his big toe.

The gruesome discovery of Willie Boy's body brought the matter to a close. But in the aftermath of the manhunt, most Indians living at the Oasis of Mara left the village for good. Some believed it was now haunted by evil spirits, but many were simply fed up with the challenge of living there. For decades the Indians at the Oasis of Mara had been involved in a bitter land dispute with Southern Pacific Railroad. Ultimately, the bad press generated by the Willie Boy incident tipped the scales in the railroad's favor. Only two Indians, an elderly couple named Jim and Matilda Pine, refused to leave the village, insisting on spending their final days near the graves of their children. By 1912, however, the Pines were also gone.

Was Willie Boy Innocent?

Decades after the Willie Boy manhunt ended, some Willie Boy scholars concluded that the posse's story was a lie. They believed it was a posse member, not Willie Boy, who had shot Carlota. According to this theory, when Carlota could no longer keep up with Willie Boy, he tried to hide her and then lead the posse away on his own. When the posse approached Carlota's hiding spot, they saw a figure moving in the distance and fired. When they drew near, they realized they had shot Carlota. The murder of the 16-year-old girl they were trying to rescue was a disaster. To cover up the situation, the men pinned the murder on Willie Boy. Scholars point out that when Carlota's body was "discovered," it was surrounded by most of Willie Boy's supplies, including a precious canteen of water. Why Willie Boy would abandon his supplies and murder the girl he loved is indeed a mystery.

THE LEGENDARY BILL KEYS

T HE DEPARTURE OF the Indians from the Oasis of Mara marked a notable shift in the character of the region. For the next several decades, local culture would be defined entirely by white miners, cattlemen, and homesteaders. The most legendary member of this group was a man named Bill Keys, who arrived in 1910 and spent most of his life within the boundaries of Joshua Tree National Park.

Keys came to Twentynine Palms at the age of 30, having spent much of his youth wandering the Southwest. He became superintendent of the once profitable Desert Queen Mine, but shortly after his arrival the mining company he worked for went bankrupt. As compensation for backwages, Keys was offered the deed to the mine, which he gladly accepted. Before long, he had homesteaded 160 acres and built himself a nearby ranch.

Several years later, on a rare trip to Los Angeles, Keys wandered into a department store and met a young saleswoman named Frances May Lawton. In 1918 the two were married. Frances moved in with Bill at his remote ranch, and the couple started a family. The Keys children grew up in frontier conditions. There was no plumbing, no electricity, and the nearest town was a two-day wagon ride away. They were physically separated from much of the outside world and survived almost entirely on local resources.

The biggest challenge in the desert was securing a steady supply of water. Keys overcame this obstacle by damming a pond behind his ranch to create a small reservoir. He stocked the reservoir with fish, and he installed pipes that irrigated a small orchard and garden on the ranch. The family swam in the reservoir in the summer, and ice skated on it when it froze in the winter.

Bill's days were filled with hard physical labor. When he wasn't mining or ranching, he was tending to the physical upkeep of his property. Frances spent her time gardening, cooking, and tending to the animals on the ranch. The children were also responsible for a variety of chores. When they did have free time, the youngsters amused themselves mostly with their imaginations. As one of the Keys children later recalled, "Our toys were usually pieces of iron or wood."

Bill Keys was a born scavenger, a trait that served him well in the desert. Over the course of his life, he claimed 35 local mine and mill sites, many of which were simply abandoned. Often he was less interested in the mine or the mill than in whatever machinery and spare parts he could scavenge from the property. His collection of odds and ends was legendary. Whenever local settlers needed spare parts, they would always turn to Keys, who accepted cash but preferred trading for more spare parts.

Bill Keys

Worth Bagley Tombstone

GUNFIGHT IN JOSHUA TREE

BILL KEYS GOT along well with most of his neighbors, but local tensions sometimes flared. Most disputes involved the desert's limited resources, and most were settled far away from the eyes of the law. In 1929 Keys shot and wounded a local cowboy over a contested water well. Following the incident, Keys developed a mixed reputation in the region. Although many knew Keys as a fair and honest man, those who crashed heads with him understood that his good nature had its breaking point.

About a decade after the incident at the well, Keys found himself involved in another feud. This one was with a retired Los Angeles Sheriff named Worth Bagley, who had moved to the region for supposed health reasons around 1938. In reality, Bagley had been discharged from the police force for his repeated abuses of power and questionable sanity. Following his arrival in Joshua Tree, he developed a reputation as a loose cannon who was constantly armed and usually angry. Before long his anger was directed at his nearest neighbor: Bill Keys.

Among other things, Bagley claimed that Keys' "vicious" cattle were constantly bothering him. When Keys found some of his cattle shot, he blamed the killings on Bagley. Bagley responded by telling Keys, "You've accused me of shooting your cattle. Don't never accuse me of that again or the next time I shoot, it won't be cattle."

The greatest point of contention between the two men involved a formerly public road that passed over part of Bagley's property. Although Keys had used the road for years, Bagley told him to stop using it. Keys repeatedly ignored him, and eventually the two men grew so angry with each other that they stopped talking entirely. Bagley was reduced to blocking the road with fallen Joshua trees and sprinkling it with broken glass.

On May 11, 1943, Keys was driving along the public section of Bagley's road when he came upon a sign that read "Keys, this is my last warning. Stay off my property." He looked up and saw Bagley approaching in the distance with a revolver. Keys grabbed his rifle but waited for Bagley to fire the first shot. Bagley fired and missed. Keys fired three shots back and Bagley's body fell to the ground.

Later that day, Keys drove to Twentynine Palms and notified local authorities of the killing. Seven weeks later Keys was brought to trial. The prosecution argued that Keys had deliberately murdered Bagley and tampered with the evidence. A doctor testified that Bagley had been shot while running away, invalidating Keys' claim of self-defense. At the end of the trail, Keys was convicted of manslaughter. He was 64 years old. The judge sentenced him to 10 years in San Quentin Prison.

Following Keys' conviction, his wife Frances devoted herself full-time to obtaining a pardon for her husband. But the family's resources were limited, and her attempts accomplished little. In desperation, Frances wrote a letter to one of Bill's old friends, a lawyer named Erle Stanley Gardner. Keys and Gardner had met in the late 1920s when Gardner came to Joshua Tree to camp. Later, Gardner started writing legal thrillers based on a fictional character named Perry Mason. The books became best-sellers, and Gardner used his celebrity to start a magazine column called "The Court of Last Resort." The column featured case histories of potentially innocent men who might have been wrongly convicted. After Gardner presented the evidence, readers would decide whether the case should be handed over to a volunteer panel of experts who would then further investigate the case.

By the time Gardner profiled Keys' case in his column, Keys had already spent four years in jail. Following publication of the article, Gardner was flooded with letters demanding that the case be reviewed. A team of experts reexamined the case and gathered a mountain of evidence to exonerate Keys. The evidence was presented to the state, which granted Keys a full pardon.

Five and a half years after Bill Keys entered prison, he walked out a free and vindicated man. He later referred to his time in prison as his "education" because he spent his days reading, catching up on current affairs, and learning how to play the guitar. Keys lived and worked at his Desert Queen Ranch for the rest of his life, becoming something of a local celebrity in his later years. His grizzled looks, checkered past, and friendly disposition gave him the aura of a Grandpa of the Old West.

In 1963 Frances Keys passed away and was buried at the Desert Queen Ranch. Six years later, Bill was laid to rest beside her. The couple had spent the better part of their lives in Joshua Tree, developing a bond with the surroundings that would probably never be surpassed by another white couple. It was in this stark landscape that Bill Keys carved out his own unique life, guided by his own principles and rugged sense of identity. As Bill's son Willis put it:

> Dad was friendly and liked to get along with people, but had a lot of poor experiences with some people, and he wouldn't let anyone run over him. He said, 'Well, if the law won't uphold me, I'll uphold myself.' And he did. He liked nature, and anybody that liked nature, he liked them. He liked the open country, and he liked fairness.

When Walt Disney Studios came to Joshua Tree in the early 1960s to film *The Wild Burro of the West*, the director was so taken with Bill Keys' grizzled looks that he offered him a walk-on role as an old prospector.

Desert Queen Ranch

Minerva Hoyt

MRS. HOYT'S MONUMENT

OVER THE COURSE of his life, Bill Keys watched the region around him change dramatically. In 1910, when he first arrived in Joshua Tree, the desert was still a remote and wild place. Although it had been discovered by white explorers several decades earlier, permanent white settlers were few and far between. Twentynine Palms was a cluster of shacks, the most advanced form of transportation was the mule-drawn wagon train, and the closest town was a two-day wagon ride away.

People drawn to this kind of environment were usually gold miners, cattle ranchers, or tuberculosis victims hoping the dry air would improve their health. But as the century progressed, this motley demographic began to change. Thanks in large part to air conditioning, the desert soon became the realm of ordinary, everyday people. By the end of the century, parts of the desert were among the fastest growing regions in California, with golf courses and strip malls claiming vast stretches of unlikely terrain.

The civilization—and later, suburbanization—of the desert traces its roots to a confluence of events in the early 1900s. When the century began, the population of Southern California was exploding. Railroads, which initially serviced only Northern California, now provided Southern California with a link to the population centers of the East. Thousands of people moved to Los Angeles in search of warm weather and cheap real estate. When the Panama Canal opened in 1914, Los Angeles became the busiest harbor on the West Coast, and the city's economy boomed. The population of Los Angeles reached 1 million in 1920, then doubled over the following decade.

As Los Angeles boomed, city sprawl edged closer to the desert. At the same time, the city's residents were unleashed by the introduction of the automobile. Suddenly, ordinary citizens had a safe, dependable way to explore the desert. Day trips became common, and newspapers published motorlogues filled with maps and detailed information.

But the desert's newfound popularity soon caused unforeseen problems. In the 1920s a gardening fad for exotic desert plants developed in Los Angeles, and enterprising landscapers began making frequent trips to the desert and uprooting plants by the truckload. Their impact was swift and dramatic. A popular destination called Devil's Garden, located just south of Joshua Tree, was filled with thousands of yucca and cacti at the turn of the century. By 1930 it had been stripped bare. Even today the plant life has yet to fully recover.

Other destructive trends were also taking place. Early desert travelers developed a habit of setting Joshua Trees on fire at night as a guide for other motorists. In 1930 the tallest known Joshua tree, which rose over 30 feet high, was set on fire and destroyed.

Minerva Hoyt's Desert Conservation Exhibit

While some citizens were reveling in their conquest of the desert, others were growing alarmed. Among the most concerned was a wealthy Pasadena widow named Minerva Hoyt. An active gardener, Hoyt had become fascinated with the desert and its beautiful plants after moving to Southern California from Mississippi in the 1890s. Following the deaths of her husband and infant son, the desert became a source of solace to Hoyt. By the 1920s she was making frequent trips to the Joshua Tree region.

On her trips to the desert, Hoyt witnessed firsthand the ecological damage that was being done. Worried that the trend would continue, she took an active role in educating citizens about desert ecosystems. In 1927 she designed a desert conservation exhibit for the Garden Club of America's flower show in New York City. The exhibit contained live cacti and stuffed animals in front of painted desert scenes, and it won the show's gold medal. At the close of the show, Hoyt donated the plants to the New York Botanical Gardens "to be preserved as museum pieces and where it would reach the greatest number of school children to teach them to know and to love the plants that it is now so necessary to conserve." She followed this up with a similar exhibit at the Royal Botanical Gardens in England two years later.

After returning from England, Hoyt was elected president of the newly organized Desert Conservation League. At the helm of this organization, she championed the creation of an extensive federal park in Southern California, encompassing parts of both the Mojave and Sonoran Deserts. She particularly liked the region just south of Twentynine Palms. But when Hoyt approached the National Park Service with her idea, she ran headfirst into a legal and bureaucratic nightmare. The boundaries outlined in her proposal were checkered with existing mining claims and plots of privately owned land. If a park was to be created, these properties would have to be purchased or accommodated. President Herbert Hoover, struggling with the Great Depression and already in a bitter land policy dispute with Congress, had little interest in tackling such a political powder keg. For the moment, Hoyt's grand idea would have to wait.

In 1932 Franklin Roosevelt was elected President. Shortly thereafter he introduced the New Deal, which was a boon to the National Park Service. Public works projects were encouraged as a way to create jobs and stimulate the lackluster economy. New park proposals were welcomed, and Harold Ickes, Roosevelt's Secretary of the Interior, supported a policy of setting aside land and working out the ownership problems later. Hoyt suddenly found herself with the perfect opportunity to promote a desert park, and she re-pitched her proposal. This time it was well received. In 1933 roughly 1 million acres of California desert were withdrawn from the public domain to be considered for National Monument status.

On August 10, 1936, Roosevelt signed a proclamation establishing Joshua Tree National Monument. Joshua Tree contained 825,000 acres of land—less than Hoyt originally wanted, but an impressive accomplishment nonetheless. Hoyt had wanted the boundaries of the new park to stretch all the way south to the Salton Sea, but the presence of the Los Angeles Metropolitan Aqueduct, which runs from the Colorado River to Los Angeles just south of the current park boundaries, prevented this from happening.

Although Hoyt had hoped for a national park rather than a slightly less protected national monument, the park service felt the area lacked any "distinctive, superlative, outstanding feature that would give it sufficient national importance to justify its establishment as a national park." The park service would ultimately reconsider its initial assessment, but for the moment the new national monument had larger problems to contend with.

Although Joshua Tree National Monument existed in name, its actual real estate remained somewhat questionable. When the monument was established, roughly 300,000 of its 825,000 acres were still privately owned. In fact, there was more private property lying within the boundaries of Joshua Tree than in the rest of the National Park Service's holdings combined, with the notable exception of Hoover Dam. And the majority of the privately owned land in Joshua Tree belonged to one owner: Southern Pacific Railroad. Aware of the newfound value of its real estate holdings, the railroad held out for the highest price.

Further complicating matters were Joshua Tree's 8,000 existing mining claims. Although new claims were now prohibited, existing mines still churned out vast quantities of gold, silver, copper, and iron ore. When the monument was established, mining companies were still extracting roughly 100 tons of ore from Joshua Tree *each day*. Although most mines operated in the remote eastern half of the monument, it was no secret that the government wanted them gone.

Over the next several decades the park service made small but effective strides in acquiring land. They patiently purchased real estate, negotiated trades, and scoured the fine print of existing deeds to find technicalities to invalidate mining claims. In a shrewd administrative maneuver, construction of a private road system was delayed to discourage private development. Then, during World War II, the government banned all gold mining in the United States due to a shortage of labor and strategic materials. Mines in Joshua Tree sat idle for years, and many fell into severe disrepair. By the time the ban was lifted, some of the mines had become unprofitable to operate. Many were abandoned and reclaimed by the government. Slowly but surely, Joshua Tree National Monument started to take shape.

CREATING A NATIONAL PARK

BY 1950 THE National Park Service had acquired enough real estate to turn Joshua Tree National Monument into a reality. But its existence was tenuous at best. A new generation of corporate prospectors, armed with new mining technologies, were eyeing the monument's vast mineral resources. Mining interests lobbied hard to open up sections of Joshua Tree to mining or, better yet, do away with the monument entirely. Their campaign was so aggressive that some people worried the monument might actually be dissolved. To prevent that from happening, the park service decided to compromise.

In 1950 280,000 acres of Joshua Tree National Monument were returned to the public domain. The land could once again be legally mined. For the park service, it was a reluctant transfer. But politically minded conservationists were determined to one day reclaim the land.

In 1964 Congress passed the Wilderness Act, which authorized the establishment of federally managed lands where mechanized vehicles and equipment were not permitted. Wilderness, according to the act, was an area "where the earth and its community of life are untrammeled by man, where man himself is a visitor who does not remain." Twelve years after the act passed, roughly 80 percent of Joshua Tree National Monument was designated wilderness, giving it an additional layer of protection. Around this time, a coalition of volunteers, legislators, and conservationists began discussing plans for sweeping legislation

President Bill Clinton signs the Desert Protection Act

that would protect vast stretches of the California desert.

In 1986 California Senator Alan Cranston introduced a desert protection bill that would transfer several million acres of land to the National Park Service. It was hardly an easy sell. The bill ignited a fierce debate in Congress over the best way to protect California's deserts, and the debate dragged on for years. By the time the act finally reached the U.S. Senate, three different Presidents had occupied the White House and Senator Cranston had been replaced by Dianne Fienstein. When the vote was finally tallied, the act had squeaked through the Senate without a single vote to spare.

On October 31, 1994, President Bill Clinton signed the Desert Protection Act. It transferred 3 million acres of land to the National Park Service, including 234,000 to Joshua Tree, which was upgraded to national park status. The remaining land went to Death Valley (also upgraded to a national park) and the newly created Mojave National Preserve, which lay between Joshua Tree and Death Valley. In its entirety, the Desert Protection Act protects the largest park and wilderness area in the lower 48 states.

Today, Joshua Tree lures over one million visitors each year. Its rugged beauty, endless opportunities for outdoor recreation, and close proximity to the largest cities in the Southwest have all contributed to its popularity, which will undoubtedly help to protect it in the years to come.

ROCK STARS & JOSHUA TREE

U2

No band will ever be as closely identified with the Joshua tree as U2. Their 1987 album, *The Joshua Tree*, is a rock masterpiece. It sold over 20 million copies and pretty much single-handedly made the band (and the trees) world famous. That four guys from Dublin could so brilliantly capture the mythology of the American desert is, frankly, a little disturbing. But our hats go off to them. Lyrics on *The Joshua Tree* are full of desert imagery—desert roses, desert skies, dust clouds, thunder storms—but strangely, Joshua trees are never mentioned. In fact, U2's connection to Joshua Tree National Park is tenuous at best. The iconic Joshua tree on their album cover was actually located north of the park, closer to Death Valley. The band was originally going to call their album *The Desert Songs* or *The Two Americas*, until cover photographer Anton Corbjin told Bono about some strange plants he'd seen in the desert called Joshua trees. The next morning Bono came down with a bible and declared that the album *had* to be called The Joshua Tree. The group drove out to the desert, located a suitable tree, and shot the cover. Bono later admitted to a friend, "it was freezing and we had to take our coats off so it would at least *look* like a desert. That's one of the reasons we look so grim." Sadly, the lone Joshua tree featured on U2's album cover has since toppled over. The location of the tree, off Route 190, is marked by rocks spelling out "U2" placed by devoted fans.

GRAM PARSONS

In 1973 the stolen corpse of country rocker Gram Parsons was smuggled into Joshua Tree National Monument and set on fire near Cap Rock. The events leading up to that incident have since become one of the classic legends of Rock n' Roll.

Parsons was a southern-bred Harvard dropout who became one of Country Music's bright young stars in the late 1960s. Many consider him to be the original alt-country crossover artist. Although his songs were country, he lived life like a rock star—flashy clothes, constant partying, heavy drinking and drug use. He became best friends with Keith Richards (Mick Jagger was reportedly extremely jealous of Gram), and the two often drove to Joshua Tree to get high, commune with nature, and scan the sky for UFOs. Before long, Gram was making regular trips to the desert.

On September 19, 1973, at the age of 26, Parsons died of a lethal combination of whiskey and morphine at the Joshua Tree Inn. His body was brought to Los Angeles to be flown back to Louisiana at the request of his stepfather, who wanted a private funeral without any of Gram's friends. As Parson's body rested in a morgue awaiting shipment, two of his friends got drunk and plotted to steal it. Parsons had once mentioned that he wanted his ashes spread in Joshua Tree, and his friends were determined to fulfill his wish. They borrowed a run-down hearse, drove to LAX, and intercepted the coffin before it was loaded onto the plane. Posing as undertakers, they convinced the airport to hand over Parson's body. After their beer and Jack Daniels-filled hearse cleared airport security, they high-tailed it to Joshua Tree. When they reached a spot near Cap Rock, they unloaded the coffin, doused it with gasoline, and set it on fire.

In the years since Parson's death, he has developed a strong cult following. His story has spawned a documentary, *Fallen Angel*, and an indie film, *Grand Theft Parsons*, starring Johnny Knoxville. Gramfest, an annual tribute to the late rocker, is held in the town of Joshua Tree each fall.

MOJAVE DESERT

★ ★ ★ ★ ★

Introduction 123
Map 124
Sights 126
Hiking 174

MOJAVE DESERT

DRIVE THROUGH THE Mojave half of the park when the sun is low and the shadows are long, and you'll feel like you've entered a lavish dreamscape. Broad valleys stretch out for miles between crumbling mountains. Vast forests of Joshua trees twist themselves into thousands of impossible shapes. Across the expanse, boulder piles as large as twenty-story buildings tower over the scenery, dwarfing everything around them except one another. Add a full moon and howling coyotes, and the terrain becomes phantasmagorical.

The Mojave is the smallest of North America's four deserts, but it's one of the most intriguing places in the world. Sandwiched between the Great Basin Desert to the north and the Sonoran Desert to the south, the Mojave is a physical transition zone that plays host to an incredible diversity of landscapes. But for all of the Mojave's strange contours and curiosities, this southern outpost remains one of its most fascinating pieces of real estate. Joshua Tree's elevation, roughly 4,000 feet above sea level, is a stark contrast to Death Valley in the northern Mojave, which at 282 feet *below* sea level marks the lowest, hottest point in North America. The higher elevation in Joshua Tree results in a relatively cooler, wetter climate where thousands of years of additional moisture have helped shape the bizarre geology of the park, sculpting surreal boulder formations that tower over the parched landscape.

But take away the bold, dramatic shapes and there remains another, more subtle realm of the desert. A place where small clusters of cacti bloom in the cracks of rocks and lizards scamper across the ground at speeds topping 20 miles per hour. A place where some plants and animals have grown entirely dependent upon one another for survival, while others have developed deadly toxins to fend each other off. This is the pulse of the desert, the space where the ecological carnival known as the Mojave Desert puts on some of its finest displays. It's easy to appreciate the landscape from a distance. But look close, and you'll find another world as captivating as any sweeping view.

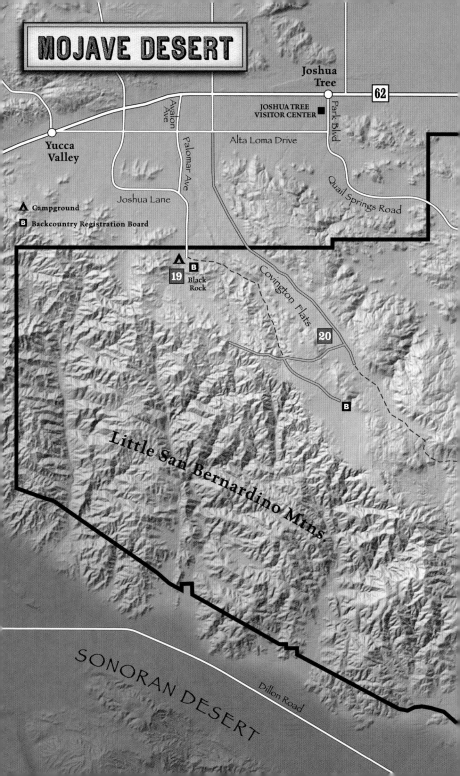

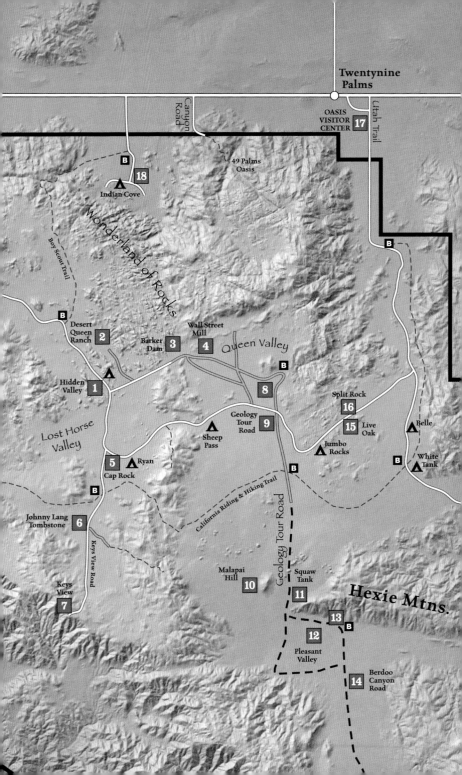

Twentynine
Palms

OASIS
VISITOR
CENTER **17**

Utah Trail

Canyon Road

49 Palms
Oasis

B

18
Indian Cove

Wonderland of Rocks

Boy Scout Trail

B

B

Desert
Queen
Ranch **2**

Barker
Dam **3**

Wall Street
Mill **4**

Queen Valley

B

8

Split Rock
16

15 Live
Oak

Belle

Hidden
Valley **1**

Geology
Tour Road **9**

Sheep
Pass

Jumbo
Rocks

White
Tank

B

Lost Horse
Valley

5
Cap Rock

Ryan

California Riding & Hiking Trail

B

B

Johnny Lang
Tombstone **6**

Keys View Road

Geology Tour Road

Malapai
Hill **10**

Squaw
Tank

11

Hexie Mtns.

Keys
View **7**

13

B

12

Pleasant
Valley

Berdoo
Canyon
Road **14**

1 Hidden Valley

This fantastic jumble of rocks shelters a peaceful valley enclosed by towering rock formations. An easy, 1-mile trail loops around Hidden Valley, and it might just be the best nature trail in the park. The trail starts to the left of the restrooms in the parking area and heads through a narrow passage in the rocks. (This opening was blasted through the rocks by local resident Bill Keys in 1936, just months before Joshua Tree National Monument was established.) Once inside the enclosed rock formation, the trail wanders the inside perimeter in a counterclockwise loop. Keep your eyes out for the steely gaze of The Trojan (above), which bears an uncanny resemblance to USC's mascot. The Trojan is located on the right shortly after starting the trail.

According to local lore, in the late 1800s two outlaw brothers named Charlie and Willie Button were wandering among the boulders here when they discovered a narrow passage in the rocks. After climbing through the passage, they discovered a secret valley enclosed by towering rock formations. Charlie had just finished a 16-year prison sentence for double murder, and he was friends with local cattle thief Bill McHaney. Before long, the Button brothers and Bill McHaney were using the secret valley as a hiding place for stolen cattle. The cattle were stolen in Arizona, brought to Hidden Valley, then re-branded and sold to unsuspecting ranchers on the California coast. Years later, both Charlie and Willie Button were killed in a barroom brawl.

3 | Barker Dam

The 1.3-mile Barker Dam loop trail winds through dramatic rock canyons and pristine valleys at the southern edge of the Wonderland of Rocks. In wet years, Barker Dam holds back a small, beautiful pond. In dry years the pond is often dry.

From the Barker Dam parking area follow the trail through narrow rock formations until you reach the dam. When cattle ranchers arrived here in the late 1800s, they found a small pool where runoff collected. By damming the far end of the pool, they created a pond for thirsty cattle. These days the pond is an important source of water for wildlife, which are best viewed in the early morning. Bighorn sheep and migrating birds like great blue herons are just some of the animals you might encounter here. From the dam, follow the trail into Piano Valley, named for a piano that was sometimes placed on the flat rock in the center of the valley to entertain camping groups from Palm Springs in the 1950s.

One of the most interesting features in Piano Valley is a rock overhang filled with Indian petroglyphs. The dramatic shapes and figures look like they could have been painted by a Hollywood movie crew—which, in fact, they were. In the 1960s a movie was shot in Joshua Tree that required a scene with dramatic Indian petroglyphs. Although the movie crew liked the authentic petroglyphs, they felt they were too understated, so they painted over them to make them show up better on film. They probably also added some primitive-looking designs of their own. Today the semi-faux petroglyphs are considered a tragic loss of the park's authentic Indian heritage.

4 Wall Street Mill

The Wall Street Mill is a weathered example of the machinery used by gold miners to process ore in the early 1900s. Although it has sat idle for decades, it is one of the best-preserved mills in the park, landing it on the National Register of Historic Sites.

The history of this mill begins in 1928, when two ambitious miners struck gold nearby. They filed their claim as "Wall Street" after the nation's then-skyrocketing money machine. The name was all too appropriate. Two years later, both the stock market and the mine were in shambles. The mine produced virtually no gold, and it was ultimately abandoned. Shortly thereafter, local resident and legendary scavenger Bill Keys reclaimed the land. He built a bunkhouse on the property and hauled in a two-stamp mill. For the next three decades, he used the Wall Street Mill to process ore from other mines. Throughout the 1930s, the Great Depression lured a steady stream of men to the desert in search of gold, and there was steady demand for processed ore. Keys charged $5 a ton to process ore, and the mill could process over two tons of ore each day.

To get to the Wall Street Mill, follow Barker Dam Road past the Barker Dam parking area and take the next road left. The easy trail starts from the north end of the parking area. Shortly after the start, the trail forks. Following it to the left takes you past the remains of a crumbling house and some rusting automobiles; continuing straight ahead takes you to the Wall Street Mill, passing an old windmill and the tombstone of Worth Bagley (p.109) along the way.

Most park visitors assume Joshua trees are cacti, but they are actually giant members of the agave family. Growing at a rate of about ½ inch per year, the largest Joshua trees can reach heights of 40 feet or more.

5 Cap Rock Nature Trail

Cap Rock Nature Trail is located to your left shortly after turning onto Keys View Road. Of all the nature trails in the park, this one definitely gives you the most bang for your buck. Short? Yes. Sweet? Definitely. Easy? Exquisitely so. A flat, wheelchair-accessible trail winds through the fantastic boulder formations while interpretive signs offer scattered desert facts along the way. If you've wanted to explore some of the park's famous boulder piles up close, but lack the time or energy to hike to some of the more remote examples, Cap Rock Nature Trail is perfect for you.

Cap Rock is named for the broad, flat boulder perched on top of the outcrop near the parking area. It's a fine example of how erosion has capriciously shaped the rocks in the park. Millions of years ago, Cap Rock and the rocks below it were all part of the same mass of granite. But as water eroded the rock along natural cracks, individual chunks separated and settled on top of one another. As the rocks continue to erode over the coming centuries, Cap Rock will either topple over or wither away. But many other interesting rock formations will undoubtedly replace it in the years to come.

In recent years, Cap Rock has attracted fans of late country rocker Gram Parsons. In 1973 Parsons died of a drug overdose in a motel just outside the park. His friends, fulfilling his final wishes, brought his body to Joshua Tree and set it on fire near Cap Rock. For more on this fascinating story, see page 119.

JOHNNY LANG

JOHN LANG
DIED HERE
BURIED BY THE
KEYS FAMILY
WHO FOUND
HIM DEAD MAR
25. 1925

6 Johnny Lang Tombstone

This lonely tombstone marks the final resting place of Johnny Lang, a shifty local prospector whose final days in Joshua Tree played out like a bumbling character from a Hollywood Western.

Lang was born in Texas in 1850, but he spent his youth as a cattle rancher in New Mexico. After his brother and six fellow cowboys were gunned down, Lang moved west and ended up at a mining camp in Joshua Tree in 1893. One fateful day Lang's horse wandered away from camp, and he followed the animal's tracks to the home of local outlaw and known cattle thief Jim McHaney. When Lang asked McHaney if he had seen his horse, McHaney looked him in the eye and explained that his horse was "no longer lost." He then told Lang to get lost.

Dejected and horseless, Lang headed to the nearby home of Frank Diebold, another struggling prospector. As the story goes, Diebold told Lang of a secret gold strike he had recently discovered but was unable to claim due to harassment from McHaney. Whenever Diebold would try to go anywhere near the strike, McHaney would chase him away. Smelling opportunity and a chance at revenge, Lang bought the rights to the strike for $1,000 and immediately took on partners to help fend off McHaney. When the strike was registered, Lang named it "Lost Horse Claim."

Lost Horse went on to become one of Joshua Tree's most profitable gold mines, ultimately producing 10,000 ounces of gold and 16,000 ounces of silver. But with so much money flowing out of the mine—millions of dollars by today's standards—robbery was a constant threat. The partners took great pains to disguise the 200-pound gold bricks they shipped to nearby towns. Unknown to the partners, however, gold was being stolen before it ever left the mine. Eventually Lang's partners noticed that the amount of gold produced by the night shift, supervised by Lang, was consistently smaller than the amount of gold produced during the day. Suspecting Lang was the culprit, the partners spied on his shift and found Lang secretly pocketing gold.

Lang was confronted by his partners, who gave him two options: go to jail or sell his stake in the mine. Lang sold, but shortly thereafter a fault was struck and the mine ran dry. His reputation shot, Lang retired to a nearby canyon. For the next 25 years he supported himself by working a small mining claim and stealing his neighbor's cattle. But from time to time, Lang sold suspiciously large quantities of gold, leading some to suspect that he had a secret stash left over from his days at the Lost Horse Mine.

On January 25, 1925, when Lang was 75 years old, he tacked a note on his door that read, "Gone for grub. Be back soon." Three months later his partially mummified remains were found at the site of his current grave. After setting out from his cabin with nothing more than a piece of bacon and a small sack of flour, Lang froze to death in his canvas sleeping bag on a cold winter night.

7 Keys View

Perched on the crest of the Little San Bernardino Mountains, Keys View offers panoramic views of Coachella Valley and the mountains beyond. A paved walkway leads to an observation area just above the parking lot, and a half-mile trail up the ridge to the west takes you to an even better view from Inspiration Point—at 5,558 feet the third-highest peak in the park.

As California's coastal population has spilled into the deserts, Coachella Valley has become one of the fastest growing regions in the state. In the 1990s its population increased 38 percent, more than double the state average. Coachella Valley is now home to nearly half a million people, but the region's booming population, combined with the massive population on the coast, has led to increases in haze and pollution that have diminished the views at Keys Point. On clear days in decades past, visitors could see all the way to Signal Peak across the Mexican Border. Recently, however, Coachella Valley became the first urban area in Southern California to meet EPA quality goals for particulate matter, much of which has been due to successful efforts to reduce air emissions that drift in from Los Angeles Basin.

1. SALTON SEA
Larger than Lake Tahoe, 25 percent saltier than the ocean. (p.144).

2. SANTA ROSA MOUNTAINS
These steep mountains rise over 8,000 feet above the Sonoran Desert.

3. SAN ANDREAS FAULT
The most notorious faultline in the world, stretching 700 miles from the Gulf of California to the Mendocino Coast north of San Francisco (p.53).

4. PALM SPRINGS
Desert playground for the rich, the famous, and the retired. What started out as an arid refuge for tuberculosis victims at the turn of the century ultimately became a Hollywood hideaway. Wealth and status soon followed, and before long Palm Springs developed into a world-class vacation resort and golf mecca.

5. SAN JACINTO PEAK
Southern California's second-highest peak (10,800 feet).

6. MT. SAN JACINTO STATE PARK
Located several thousand feet above Coachella Valley, this alpine wilderness is filled with pine trees, campgrounds, hiking trails, and cross-country skiing in the winter. An aerial tram makes daily runs between Palm Springs and the upper reaches of the San Jacinto Mountains, rising over a vertical mile along the way.

7. SAN GORGONIO PASS
The gateway to LA and one of the windiest places in the state (p.145).

8. SAN GORGONIO PEAK
Southern California's highest peak (11,500 feet.)

Salton Sea

At 360-square miles, the Salton Sea is North America's second-largest body of saltwater after Utah's Great Salt Lake. Although created by accident nearly a century ago, it has since carved out an unlikely niche in California's modern ecosystem. In 1901 the first dam was built along the Colorado River, helping to irrigate Southern California's fertile deserts and making it possible to grow crops an amazing 12 months out of the year. But the Colorado carries an enormous amount of sediment, and in 1905 the dam silted up and the river jumped its banks. Rather than drain into the Gulf of California, the Colorado flowed into the desert lowlands south of Joshua Tree. It took three full years to redirect the river, and those three years were some of the wettest in the history of the Colorado River Basin. By the time the river was finally redirected, an inland sea nearly one-third the size of Rhode Island had formed. Interestingly, the Salton Sea formed at least twice in geologic times when the Colorado silted up and jumped its banks on its own. In those cases, however, the sea eventually evaporated after the Colorado naturally redirected itself. The Salton Sea would be drying up today if not for the massive amounts of agricultural runoff from the Imperial Valley to the south. This runoff, rich in nitrogen and phosphorous, has turned the Salton Sea into a smelly, briny, algae-rich soup—a condition that just happens to make it an ecological paradise for birds. As wetlands have disappeared along the California coast, migrating birds have found refuge at the Salton Sea, leading some experts to refer to it as a "crown jewel of avian biodiversity."

San Gorgonio Pass

This narrow notch between the Santa Rosa and San Bernardino Mountains is one of the windiest places in California. As the sun bakes the ground in the desert, hot air rises up into the atmosphere, creating a vacuum that's filled by cool air rushing in from the coast. Much of the rushing air is blocked by tall mountains, so the surge is concentrated in a few narrow gaps. San Gorgonio Pass is one of them, with wind speeds here averaging between 15 and 20 mph.

Starting in the early 1980s, with 1970s-era gas lines and OPEC price hikes fresh in people's minds, wind energy was championed as an alternative to America's dependence on foreign oil. By 1986 over 4,000 wind turbines had been installed in San Gorgonio Pass, making it the third-largest wind farm in California. When the turbines were first installed at San Gorgonio Pass, wind energy was much more expensive to produce than energy generated by fossil fuels. But recent advances in technology, combined with government subsidies, have since made wind energy far more price competitive. As older turbines have been replaced in San Gorgonio Pass, the total number of turbines has dropped while their energy output has nearly doubled. Today roughly 3,100 turbines deliver about 1,000 megawatts (MW)—about a third of California's total wind energy production. California is ranked third in the nation in wind energy production, behind Texas (9,500 MW) and Iowa (3,700 MW). Although California is a leader in wind energy development, it is only ranked 17th among U.S. states in terms of total wind-energy potential.

QUEEN VALLEY

N

To Barker
Dam

4400

Park Boulevard

Queen Valley

Geology
Tour
Road

To
Jumbo Rocks

4436'

Pine City

Desert Queen
Mine

4520'
Lucky Boy
Vista

8 Queen Valley

The dusty dirt roads that crisscross Queen Valley are overlooked by many visitors—which is a shame because Queen Valley is home to some of the park's most fantastic Joshua trees. The tallest Joshua tree in the park is found here (over 40 feet high), and there are also a handful of easy hikes, including Lucky Boy Vista (2.5 miles), Pine City (3 miles), and the Desert Queen Mine (1.2 miles).

The scattered remains of the Desert Queen Mine are a slowly decaying memorial to the turbulent, often scandalous gold-mining era that flourished here a century ago. An easy trail heads to an overlook above the mine, and a slightly more adventurous trail descends into a ravine among the ruins. To get to both, follow the trail from the parking area for about half a mile until you reach a backcountry registration board. Continuing straight takes you to the overlook, turning right leads you down into the ravine (a moderate hike).

The Desert Queen Mine traces its roots to a man named Frank L. James, who was working at the lucrative Lost Horse Mine a few miles south in the early 1880s. Determined to someday strike it rich on his own, James spent his nonworking hours scouring the desert for gold. In the spring of 1894, he struck a rich vein here. The deposits James discovered were described as "so rich in gold as to cause the most extravagant reports of the value of the mine," and news of his discovery spread like wildfire. Among those informed was a local outlaw named Jim McHaney, an unsuccessful miner whose full time job consisted of stealing cattle. On April 5, 1894 McHaney and two friends trailed James to his new strike, shot him dead, and took over the mine as their own.

The Desert Queen Mine produced a small fortune for McHaney—which he spent as quickly as possible. He bought diamond rings, a diamond belt buckle, a diamond encrusted hat, and a walking stick covered in diamonds. For two years McHaney pranced around the desert covered in jewels. But when the mine ran dry, his debts quickly caught up with him. Reduced to poverty, McHaney started counterfeiting gold coins—a crime that ultimately landed him in San Quentin Prison.

For the next quarter century the Desert Queen Mine fell in and out of favor with local prospectors as they tried to locate new pockets of gold. The mine's final scandal came in the early 1930s. At that point a jeweler named Frederick Morton met a cook from a nearby mining camp who passed himself off as a skilled mining engineer. The cook convinced Morton that he could extract vast quantities of gold from the Desert Queen Mine—provided he had adequate capital. Dreaming of riches, Morton eagerly opened his wallet. Amazingly, the cook discovered a new deposit of gold by sheer dumb luck, but he kept this discovery to himself and quietly pocketed the returns. As Morton continued to finance the mining operation, his own fortune dwindled, leading him to issue illegal stock in the mine. As the story goes, Morton was convicted of fraud while the cook and his wife took a trip around the world.

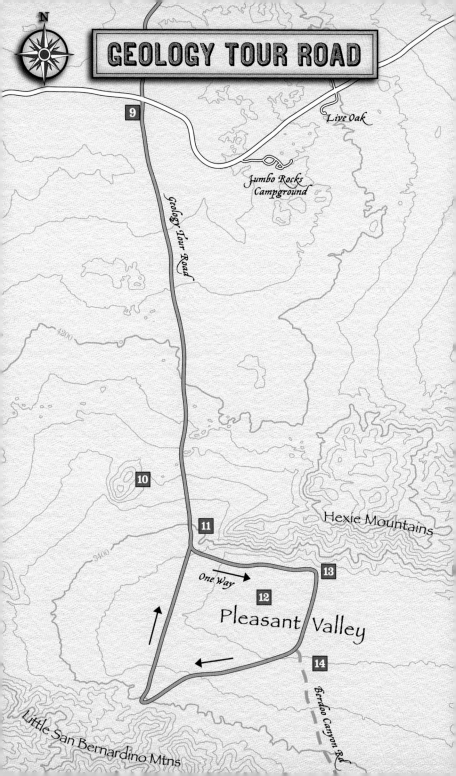

9 Geology Tour Road

This rugged, 18-mile round-trip dirt road descends over 1,000 feet to an ancient, dried-up lakebed and a broad, beautiful valley. Along the way it passes by some of the park's finest geological specimens—boulder outcrops, a volcanic hill, and dramatic eroding mountains. But even non-geologists will enjoy the prehistoric Indian campsites, abandoned gold mines, and (following wet winters) explosions of wildflowers in the spring. If you're fascinated by desert geology or just looking to get off the beaten path, the Geology Tour Road is a great destination. From start to finish, it takes about one to two hours at a leisurely pace, although geologists and rock aficionados should budget more time.

The turnoff for the Geology Tour Road is in Queen Valley, about two miles west of Jumbo Rocks Campground and six miles east of Ryan Campground. Restrooms are located near the start of the Geology Tour Road. About five miles from the start, the road becomes four-wheel drive only. Numbered signposts along the side of the road correspond to information found in a short pamphlet produced by the park. The pamphlet is available at the visitor center or from a small metal box near the start of the Geology Tour Road.

Note: The Geology Tour Road is not suitable for campers, trailers, and motor homes. Because the road is not maintained, vehicles without four-wheel-drive should only attempt the first five miles. If you do not have four-wheel-drive, do not go past Squaw Tank (stop #9). In bad weather, vehicles without four-wheel drive should avoid the Geology Tour Road entirely.

BOULDER OUTCROPS

As you drive along the Geology Tour Road, you'll pass several massive boulder outcrops. Millions of years ago, these boulders were all part of the same mass of granite, which was then buried deep underground. As erosion removed the overlying rocks, the granite neared the surface and came into contact with ground-water trickling down through the soil. The water eroded the granite along its cracks and separated it into jumbled chunks of rock. As erosion continued to remove the soil above, the chunks of rock lay exposed, ultimately settling into the fantastic boulder outcrops that you see today.

10 Malapai Hill

Around 100 million years ago, magma rose up under Joshua Tree and cooled to form the park's granite. Much later, sometime between 8 million and 100,000 years ago, new intrusions of magma rose up under the granite and cooled into black basalt. Malapai Hill formed as a result of one of these later magma intrusion, which accounts for the hill's dark coloration. When the magma rose up, however, the surrounding rocks were still buried deep underground. Geologists are unsure if the magma that formed Malapai Hill rose high enough to reach the surface. If so, Malapai Hill is part of an ancient volcano. It's also possible that the magma never broke the surface and simply cooled deep underground. Because the basalt that makes up Malapai Hill is much harder than the surrounding granite, it is much more resistant to erosion, which is why the hill towers above the rest of the landscape.

The name "Malapai" is probably derived from *malpai*, a word used by early Spanish explorers to describe the black landscape of volcanic basalt flows on the southern edge of the Colorado Plateau. Malpai is derived from the Spanish words *mal* (evil) and *pais* (country).

If you choose to explore Malapai Hill up close, keep your eyes out for Balance Rock, located near the hill's southern base. This giant boulder is balanced exquisitely on its tiny base.

13 Gold Coin Mine

These two rusting metal tanks were once used to process ore from the nearby Gold Coin Mine, located in the hills above. The mine was discovered in 1900 and was lucrative enough to be worked for the next 38 years. The tanks were used in a process called cyanide leaching, which was invented in the late 1800s and is still used today. Cyanide is one of the few solutions capable of dissolving gold, and it was poured over crushed ore in the tanks. The cyanide/gold solution was then drained and chemically separated. Cyanide leaching is extremely effective—even microscopic gold flakes can be extracted profitably from low-grade ore—but cyanide is highly toxic. One teaspoon of two percent cyanide solution can cause death in humans. As a result, its use in gold extraction remains highly controversial. Although cyanide breaks down quickly when exposed to sunlight, accidental spills can wreck havoc on fragile ecosystems.

14 Berdoo Canyon Road

This rugged, unmaintained road runs 15.4 miles between the Geology Tour Road and Dillon Road, located just south of the park. A high-clearance four-wheel-drive vehicle is required to safely navigate Berdoo Canyon Road. The last 3.9 miles of Berdoo Canyon Road pass by the ruins of Berdoo Camp, which was established in the 1930s by the builders of the California Aqueduct.

· SKULL ROCK ·

This unusual rock formation, located just east of Jumbo Rocks Campground, is famous for its vague resemblance to a human skull. The eye sockets that give Skull Rock its eerie anthropomorphism are a geological phenomenon called *tafoni*. Centuries ago, the tafoni started out as nothing more than tiny depressions in the granite. Over time, rainwater accumulated in the tiny depressions and eroded the rock. As more rock eroded, more rainwater accumulated, leading to more erosion and so on. Eventually, two large eye sockets formed. A 1.7-mile nature trail passes by Skull Rock and loops back through Jumbo Rocks Campground. This easy trail is filled with fantastic rock scenery and dotted with signs that point out scattered facts about geology and desert plants.

15 Live Oak

This small rest area has several picnic tables surrounded by dramatic rock formations. It's reached via a small dirt road that turns south off Park Boulevard just east of Skull Rock. The parking area is located just above a gravelly wash (a dry streambed where water flows when it rains), and just down the wash is the oak tree that gives Live Oak its name. The oak is a rare hybrid of the small turbinella oak (found throughout the park) and the valley oak (found in the distant San Joaquin Valley). The acorns produced by oak trees like this one provided an important source of food for Indians who once lived in the park. Be sure to check out the rock formation above the oak tree, which has been piously dubbed "The Pope's Hat."

If you follow the wash past the oak tree, you'll arrive at Ivanpah Tank. When cattle ranchers came here in the late 1800s, the most important factor affecting their success was a reliable source of water. To collect runoff, ranchers often built small dams in washes, and the small pools that formed were called "tanks."

16 Split Rock

Across the road from the Live Oak turnoff is a turnoff to Split Rock, a giant boulder weighing roughly 120 tons with a sharply defined crack splitting it in two. Several picnic tables and a restroom are located near the parking area.

17 Oasis of Mara

This fan palm oasis, located beyond the park's northern boundary in the town of Twentynine Palms, is home to the Oasis Visitor Center, which features a help desk, a bookstore, and a small museum. An outdoor garden also showcases a wide variety of desert plants found in the park, and a short self-guided nature trail wraps around the palms behind the visitor center.

Centuries before white settlers set eyes on the palms surrounding this oasis, it was the site of a village occupied by the Serrano Indians. *Mara* is a Serrano word that means "Place of Little Springs and Much Grass." Legend has it that a medicine man told the Indians to go to the oasis because they would have many boy babies if they lived there. Each time a baby boy was born, the medicine man instructed them to plant a new palm. In their first year at the oasis, the Indians planted 29 palms.

The water and resources the Serrano found at the oasis were invaluable to their survival in the desert. They built shelters out of palm fronds and hunted animals that came to the oasis to drink. When an early government expedition came here in the 1850s, they found the Indians growing corn, beans, pumpkins, and squash. When white miners and cattlemen arrived in the late 1800s, they shared the resources at the oasis with the Indians. In 1902 roughly 40 Indians lived at the oasis. But a land dispute with Southern Pacific Railroad and growing Indian mistrust among whites ultimately pressured many Indians to leave. By 1913 the Indians had abandoned their ancient village.

Oasis of Mara, Winter

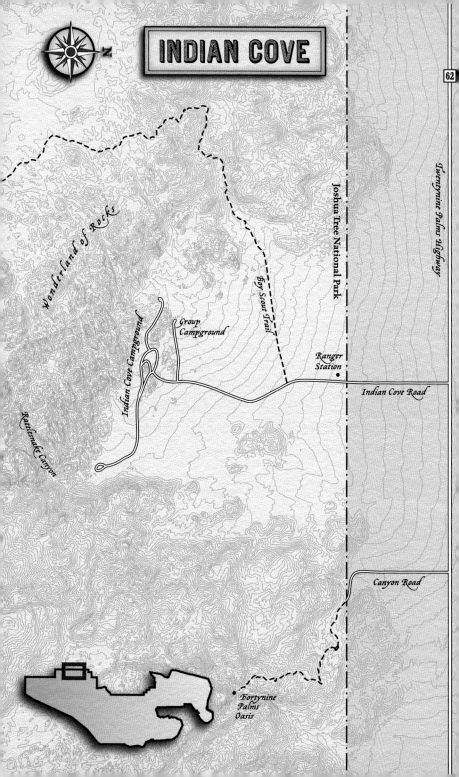

INDIAN COVE

62

Twentynine Palms Highway

Joshua Tree National Park

Wonderland of Rocks

Boy Scout Trail

Group
Campground

Indian Cove Campground

Ranger
Station

Indian Cove Road

Rattlesnake Canyon

Canyon Road

Fortynine
Palms
Oasis

18 Indian Cove

This gorgeous campground, located at the northern edge of the Wonderland of Rocks near the park's boundary, is home to some of Joshua Tree's most impressive geology. Driving in from Highway 62, you'll be treated to dramatic views of towering rock formations looming above the campground. Not surprisingly, Indian Cove is very popular with rock climbers. Its 3,200-foot elevation is several hundred feet lower than other campgrounds in the Mojave half of the park, making it slightly warmer in the cold winter months. And although Indian Cove feels relatively secluded, its close proximity to Highway 62 gives it easy access to the shops and restaurants in the nearby towns of Joshua Tree and Twentynine Palms. (See p.34 for a detailed campground map.)

Indian Cove also offers close proximity to two of the park's best hikes: 49 Palms Oasis (p.180), located just south of Indian Cove off Canyon Road, and the Boy Scout Trail (p.178), located at the backcountry board located just south of the Indian Cove ranger station. Indian Cove is also home to an easy 0.6-mile nature trail that loops through some mellow terrain at the far western end of the campground. Interpretive signs along the trail point out facts about plants, animals, and the Indians who once used this area as a seasonal camp. If you're looking for a more rugged and adventurous hike, head to Rattlesnake Canyon at the far eastern end of the campground. After scrambling up the boulder-strewn mouth of Rattlesnake Canyon, you'll reach a gorgeous slot canyon polished smooth by centuries of flash floods.

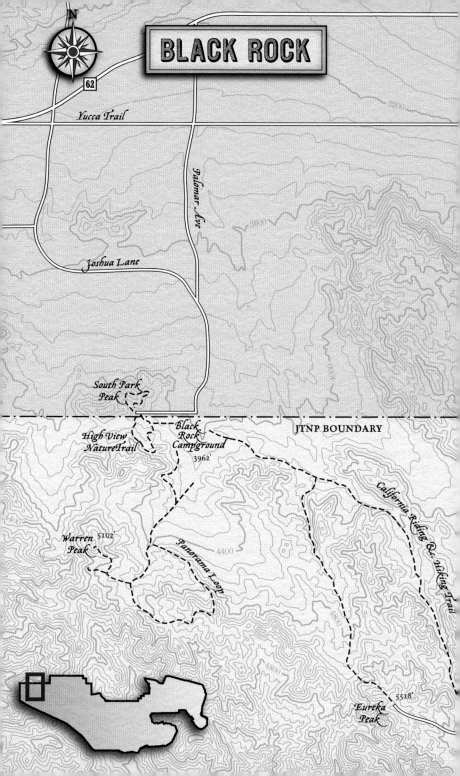

19 Black Rock

Black Rock Canyon, located in the far northwestern corner of the park, is home to a large campground with a handful of great hikes nearby. The area is also popular with horseback riders, and there's a large area for stock animals next to the campground. Like Indian Cove, Black Rock's close proximity to Highway 62 offers easy access to shops and restaurants just outside the park. The 100-site campground overlooks Yucca Valley, and at night you can see the town's lights twinkling below.

Black Rock campground is filled with Joshua trees, but the higher elevations just south of the campground are filled with juniper, pinyon pine, oak, and other plants typical of the pinon-juniper ecosystem. The vegetation gives the area a distinctly different feel from the rest of the park. It also lures a wide variety of animals. Over 200 bird species have been identified nearby, and mule deer are sometimes spotted running alongside the trails.

Hiking trails near the campground run the gamut from easy nature trails to strenuous hikes. The easy High View Nature Trail, which starts just west of the entrance to Black Rock Campground, rambles over pretty scenery in a 1.3-mile loop. Numbered posts along the trail correspond to a brochure available at the Black Rock ranger station. Adjacent to the nature trail is the South Park Peak Trail, an easy 0.8-mile loop that climbs 255-feet and offers great views of the surrounding area. If you're looking for a longer, more strenuous hike, check out Warren Peak (p.182) and the Panorama Loop.

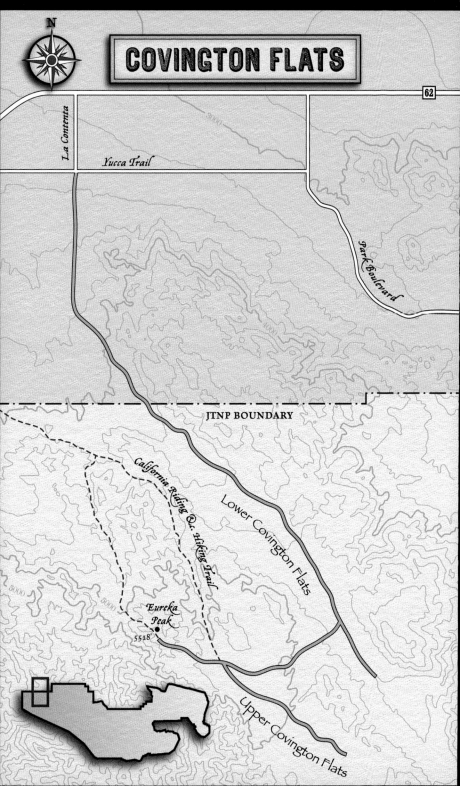

20 Covington Flats

The dirt roads that pass through Covington Flats provide relatively good access to a rugged and disconcertingly beautiful section of Joshua Tree. Here you'll find some of the largest Joshua trees, pinyon pines, and junipers in the park. The most popular destination at Covington Flats is Eureka Peak—at 5,518 feet the fourth highest peak in the park. On clear days the 360-degree views from Eureka Peak go on for miles.

   Much of the landscape here is blackened and charred from a wildfire that tore through Covington Flats following a lightning strike in 1995. By the time the fire was extinguished, it had burned over 5,000 acres. Roughly three-quarters of fires in Joshua Tree are caused by lightning strikes; the rest are caused by people. Fires are a healthy part of many ecosystems, but fires in Joshua Tree—including naturally caused fires—are much more complex. Desert ecosystems recover very slowly from fires. The shallow root systems of many desert plants burn easily, and fires destroy seeds lying on the ground waiting to germinate. Many plants require decades to fully recover from fires, and Joshua trees sometimes require hundreds of years. Before the arrival of European settlers, fires caused by lightning strikes were part of the natural desert ecosystem. But today many non-native plants, particularly grasses, have found their way into the park. These new grasses burn easily and recover quickly. Park records indicate that the number and intensity of natural fires has increased over the years. Until this problem is studied further, the National Park Service plans on suppressing all fires within the park.

～ RYAN MOUNTAIN ～

SUMMARY   Rising above some of the most spectacular scenery in the park, Ryan Mountain is one of Joshua Tree's top attractions. At 5,457 feet it's the fifth highest peak in the park, but the hike to its summit starts at 4,480 feet, which means you're only looking at 977 feet of total elevation change. The trail starts from the Ryan Mountain parking area, merges with a trail from Sheep Pass Campground, and then follows a well-traveled route to the top. The trail wraps around the craggy, northwest corner of the mountain (offering great views of Hidden Valley and the Wonderland of Rocks below) before tucking into a deep cleft as it nears the peak. Panoramic views roll down from the top, filled with broad valleys, crumbling mountains, and miles of blue sky above. On clear days the view includes Mt. San Jacinto and Mt. San Gorgonio, two of the highest peaks in Southern California.

TRAILHEAD   The Ryan Mountain Trail starts at the Ryan Mountain parking area, located just off Park Boulevard between Queen Valley and Lost Horse Valley at the base of Ryan Mountain.

TRAIL INFO

DIFFICULTY: Strenuous

DISTANCE: 3 miles, round-trip

HIKING TIME: 2–3 Hours

ELEVATION CHANGE: 977 ft.

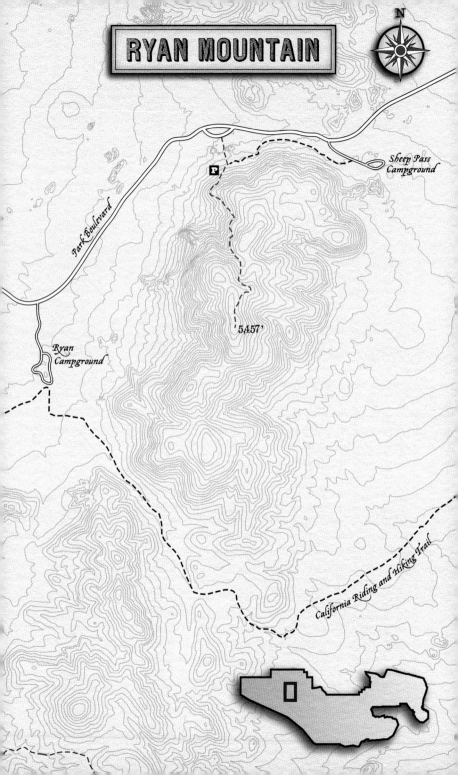

RYAN MOUNTAIN

N

Park Boulevard

Sheep Pass
Campground

P

5457'

Ryan
Campground

California Riding and Hiking Trail

⚼ LOST HORSE MINE ᵔ

SUMMARY   This pleasant hike takes you to the remains of the Lost Horse Mine, one of the most productive gold mines in the history of Joshua Tree. Between 1894 and 1942 the Lost Horse Mine produced over 10,000 ounces of gold and 16,000 ounces of silver—over $12 million by today's standards. The largest gold nugget the mine ever produced was the size of a man's fist. During the mine's heyday a small village was established nearby, and a 10-stamp mill (above) was built to process the ore. The mill was powered by a steam engine, and water was pumped up the mountainside from a well 750 feet below. Today all that remains is a plugged mineshaft and the 10-stamp mill, which has fallen into disrepair. But the hike to Lost Horse Mine is still worthwhile. Twisting through the upper reaches of the Little San Bernardino Mountains, the trail follows an old abandoned mining road.

TRAILHEAD   The trailhead is located at the end of Lost Horse Road, which turns off Keys View Road about two miles past Cap Rock.

◤ TRAIL INFO ◥

DIFFICULTY: Strenuous   **HIKING TIME:** 2–3 Hours

DISTANCE: 4 miles, round-trip   **ELEVATION CHANGE:** 480 ft.

LOST HORSE MINE

N

Park Boulevard

• Cap Rock

Ryan Campground

Ryan Mountain

California Riding and Hiking Trail

Keys View Road

P

Lost Horse • Mine

Keys View

⊸⊲ BOY SCOUT TRAIL ⊳⊶

SUMMARY This popular trail, which connects Park Boulevard to Indian Cove, is often done as a one-way hike, with one car left at the start and one car left at the finish. If you start from the Keys West Backcountry Board (located next to a small parking area just off Park Boulevard), the trail runs almost entirely downhill, skirting the western edge of the Wonderland of Rocks before tucking into a series of narrow canyons, then emerging at Indian Cove. The Boy Scout Trail is the most popular overnight hike in the park, but if you're planning an overnight trip you must camp west of the trail. The land to the east of the trail (the Wonderland of Rocks) is day-use only due to the presence of sensitive wildlife such as bighorn sheep. Also be aware of potential flash flood dangers when camping in washes.

TRAILHEAD There are two possible starting points for the Boy Scout Trial: the Keys West Backcountry Board, located 0.5 mile east of the Quail Springs Picnic Area, or the Indian Cove Backcountry Board, located just south of the Indian Cove Ranger Station.

◤ TRAIL INFO ◥

DIFFICULTY: Moderate   **HIKING TIME:** 4–5 Hours

DISTANCE: 8 miles, one-way   **ELEVATION CHANGE:** 1,345 ft.

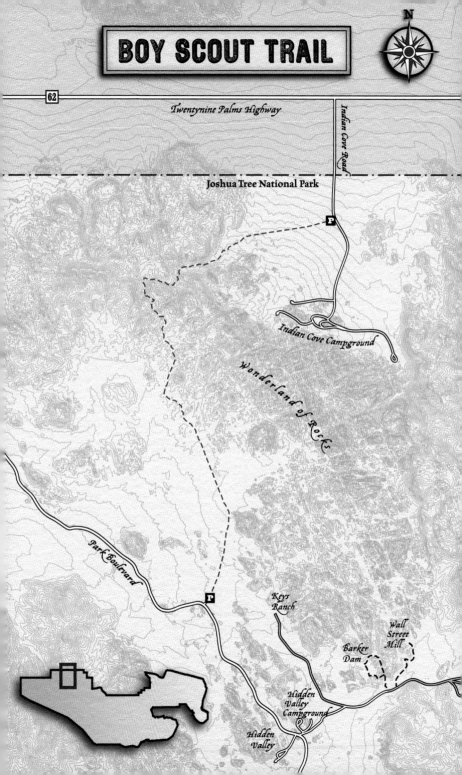

～ 49 PALMS OASIS ～

SUMMARY   This California fan palm oasis, nestled at the foot of a deep, rocky canyon, is one of the most exquisite destinations in the park. The trail that leads to the oasis is well-maintained, easy to follow, and filled with great views. From the trailhead it curves up and over a small rise before wrapping around several craggy hills as it descends towards the oasis. California fan palms live only in places where there is a steady supply of water. The natural oasis found here allows the palms to thrive. Since the 1940s, however, several fires have swept through the oasis, burning away the frond skirts and charring the trunks of many trees. But the palms not only survived the fire, they became healthier and more productive as a result. In addition to killing insects and other pests, the fires killed small plants that competed with the palms for water.

TRAILHEAD   The trail to 49 Palms Oasis starts from a parking area at the end of Canyon Road, which heads south off Highway 62 about 1.75 miles east of Indian Cove Road. (The turnoff is often easy to miss—look for a small animal hospital near the intersection of Canyon Road and Highway 62.)

TRAIL INFO

DIFFICULTY: Strenuous

DISTANCE: 3 miles, round-trip

HIKING TIME: 2–3 Hours

ELEVATION CHANGE: 360 ft.

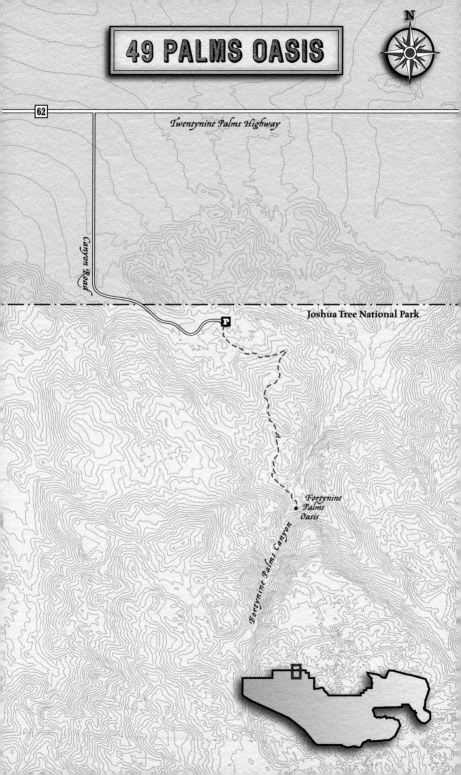

⌐◄ WARREN PEAK ►⌐

SUMMARY   At 5,102 feet, Warren Peak is the 10th highest peak in the park. A scramble to the top provides unobstructed views of the Little San Bernardino Mountains, Coachella Valley, Mt. San Jacinto, and Mt. San Gorgonio. From the trailhead at Black Rock Campground, follow the trail a short distance, then turn left onto a service road. A short distance later turn right onto a trail, then head south (right) when the trail splits. Follow the signs to Warren Peak. The majority of this trail is relatively easy; only the final approach on the eastern ridge of Warren Peak is strenuous. If you'd like to extend the hike on your return, follow the southern loop of the Panorama Trail, which offers fantastic 360-degree views of the surrounding landscape, including (on clear days) views of the Salton Sea to the southeast.

TRAILHEAD   The trail to Warren Peak starts at the southern end of Black Rock Campground, near campsite #30.

TRAIL INFO

DIFFICULTY: Strenuous

DISTANCE: 6 miles, round-trip

HIKING TIME: 4–5 Hours

ELEVATION CHANGE: 1,123 ft.

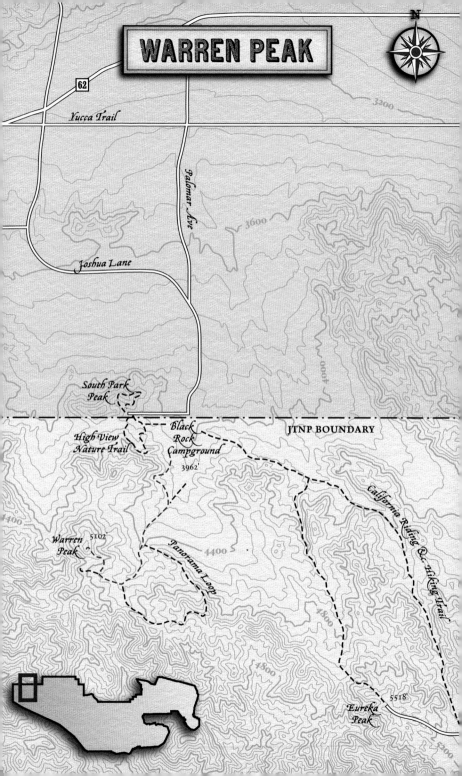

SONORAN DESERT

★ ★ ★ ★ ★

Introduction 187
Map 188
Sights 191
Hiking 208

SONORAN DESERT

ABOUT FIVE MILES south of the Oasis of Mara, Pinto Basin Road turns off Park Boulevard and heads over a slight rise. The road drifts through a small stretch of Joshua trees and boulder outcrops before dropping into a small, twisty canyon. Then, at roughly 2,700 feet, the canyon yawns open to reveal a massive gulf of land spread out below. This is Pinto Basin, the largest physical feature in the park.

Bounded by five distinct mountain ranges, Pinto Basin covers roughly 200 square miles. At nearly one-quarter the size of Rhode Island, it takes up almost half of the park. But Pinto Basin is noteworthy for more than just its physical dimensions. This massive dollop of land marks one of the western-most edges of the Sonoran Desert—a vast, continental region that stretches across Arizona, spills into Mexico, straddles the Gulf of California, and reaches down to the tip of the Baja Peninsula.

The Sonoran Desert in Southern California is also referred to as the Colorado Desert, named for the Colorado River that marks the boundary between California and Arizona. Although the Colorado Desert is the most arid region in North America, it is home to a stunning diversity of plants and animals. No other desert in the world contains a comparable variety of plants. But compared with the lurid shapes of the Mojave, the Sonoran often seems barren and minimal—a stark kind of beauty that's less Dr. Seuss and more John Wayne.

This is a harsh environment that refuses to coddle its inhabitants, and they have sharpened their survival skills accordingly. Plants and animals living in the Colorado Desert make due with a bare minimum of resources, none of which are guaranteed from one day to the next, and their evolutionary adaptations are remarkable. Kangaroo rats can go their entire lives without ever drinking a single drop of water, extracting all the liquid they need from food and recycling water again and again through super-efficient kidneys. In addition, special chambers in the kangaroo rat's nasal passages condense moisture to retain water from exhaled air. In many ways, this is nature at its finest. Evolution has overcome a deadly landscape, and life thrives despite a paucity of basic resources.

SONORAN DESERT

MOJAVE DESERT

Pinto Mtns.

62

B

B

▲ Belle

B 1 White
        ▲ Tank

▲
Jumbo
Rocks

B

2

Hexie Mtns.

3

B

4   5   Pinto Basin Road

Pinto Basin

B

Old Dale Rd.

B

B

6

Black Eagle Mine Rd.

Pinkham Canyon Rd.

Cottonwood Mtns.

7   ▲ Cottonwood
        B

1 Arch Rock Nature Trail

Before Pinto Basin Road dips down into the Sonoran Desert, it passes by White Tank Campground and Arch Rock Nature Trail. The trail starts in the campground and winds through an impressive collection of sculpted granite, similar to the famous rock outcrops found along Park Boulevard. The highlight of the trail is Arch Rock, a 25-foot natural arch formed by centuries of erosion. While much of the park's granite has crumbled upon itself, the cracks in Arch Rock were arranged in such a way that erosion left this beautiful arch behind.

Arch Rock Nature Trail starts by campsite #9. To get there, turn into White Tank Campground from Pinto Basin Road, then bear left until you reach a small parking area near the campsite. A sign marks the start of the trail, which forms a 0.3-mile counterclockwise loop. Arch Rock is located a short distance from the start of the trail.

White Tank Campground gets its name from nearby White Tank, a water reservoir built by ranchers in the early 1900s. The "White" in White Tank comes from a man named Captain White, who was involved with a nearby gold mine. When geologists first studied the rock formations in Joshua Tree, they started with the ones found here. As a result, the specific type of granite that Arch Rock Nature Trail passes through is named White Tank Quartz Monzogranite.

Silver Bell Mine

2 Wilson Canyon

After passing White Tank Campground, Pinto Basin Road drops into Wilson Canyon, which lies along the western edge of the Hexie Mountains. Brittle, weather-beaten hills line both sides of the road. Though stark and forbidding for much of the year, the landscape here often explodes with wildflowers in the spring. After passing through Wilson Canyon, you'll enter the Sonoran Desert.

The boundaries of North America's four great deserts—the Mojave, Sonoran, Great Basin, and Chihuahuan—were established by an Arizona ecologist named Forest Shreve. In the early 1900s Shreve separated the entire North American desert into four subdivisions based on elevation, vegetation, and precipitation. He then further divided the Sonoran into seven distinct vegetative regions, including the Colorado Desert in Southern California. Because the boundaries of these four great deserts are based on a combination of complex factors, they are often fuzzy and imprecise. Wilson Canyon lies in one of those fuzzy boundaries where the Mojave gradually blends into the Sonoran.

As you descend into the Sonoran Desert, you'll discover a landscape dominated by creosote bushes (p.72), with scattered patches of other desert plants such as cholla, ocotillo, smoke trees, and palo verde. Because the desert is lower and hotter here, this part of Joshua Tree National Park experiences the first wildflower blooms in the spring.

3 Silver Bell Mine

After passing through Wilson Canyon, look for a pullout on the right side of the road with a sign that describes the Silver Bell Mine. The remains of this abandoned mine can be seen in the hills above—look for two large wooden bins near the crest of the hills to the west. These wooden bins, called "tipples," were used to store ore extracted from the Silver Bell Mine.

The Silver Bell Mine was one of nearly 300 mines that operated within the current boundaries of the park from the late 1800s to the mid-1900s. Although gold was by far the most prized metal, miners also searched for silver, copper, and other metals. The Silver Bell Mine operated from the 1930s to the 1960s. During that time it produced at least 219 ounces of gold and 53 ounces of silver, worth over $200,000 today. Copper was also extracted from the Silver Bell Mine, and during World War II it was converted into a lead mine.

Although no official trail leads to the Silver Bell Mine, it's possible to see the remains up close if you don't mind some desert scrambling. After crossing over the gravelly flats, follow an old, obvious mining road to the remains of the mine. Remember: use extreme caution near abandoned mines in Joshua Tree. Many mines have open shafts that drop hundreds of feet.

Pinto Basin

This enormous, 200-square-mile basin gets its name from the Pinto Mountains that appear to your left as you travel down the road. Early explorers named these multicolored mountains after the multicolored pinto horse. (The word pinto means "mottled" and is derived from Spanish words such as *pintor,* "painter," and *pintoresco,* "picturesque" or "colorful.")

Pinto Basin formed when the surrounding mountains were uplifted along fault lines and the land between them dropped. As erosion slowly chips away at the mountains, loose debris tumbles down their slopes. But because there are no streams to carry away the debris, it slowly spreads out over Pinto Basin, creating a broad, flat landscape. If the landscape were located in a more humid climate, vegetation growing on the mountain slopes would reduce erosion and flowing streams would cut deep valleys between the mountains.

As you drive through Pinto Basin, look for alluvial fans (sloping debris piles) spreading out from canyons at the base of the mountains. Some geologists believe these alluvial fans formed at the end of the last Ice Age. As the climate dried out, Ice Age vegetation disappeared from the mountains, and soil that had formed on the slopes was carried down by runoff. Today when runoff rushes down the mountains, it picks up sediments in the alluvial fans and slowly spreads them out. As the alluvial fans spread out they often merge, forming *bajadas.*

In the 1920s an amateur archaeologist name Elizabeth Campbell was exploring Pinto Basin when she discovered stone projectile points scattered across the ground. These primitive tools, fashioned several thousand years ago, provided the first known evidence of human habitation in the park. Campbell gathered as many artifacts as she could and later donated her collection to the park. Some of these primitive tools are now on display at the Oasis Visitor Center.

Where are the Cacti?

The Sonoran Desert is famous for its tall, green Saguaro Cacti (often pictured wearing sombreros and wielding six-shooters on Mexican restaurant signs), but Saguaros are notably absent from the Sonoran Desert in California—aka the Colorado Desert. Because of the Colorado Desert's low elevations and relative lack of summer rain, it's hotter and drier than the rest of the Sonoran. As a result, plants that require ample moisture, such as Saguaros, are unable to survive here.

4 Cholla Cactus Garden

This surreal cactus patch is one of the most interesting destinations in the park. One moment you're casually driving into Pinto Basin, the next you're surrounded by a goonish army of lanky, gangly, multicolored, fuzzy-looking cacti. To observe these bizarre cacti up close, pull into the small parking area on the right side of the road. An easy 0.3-mile nature trail starts from the parking area and winds through the cacti, and a fact-filled pamphlet is available in a box near the start of the trail.

Most plants have one or two common names. These cacti, *Opuntia bigelovii*, have three: Bigelow Cholla (from its scientific name), Teddybear Cholla (because it looks like some kind of fuzzy, nightmarish teddybear), and Jumping Cholla (because its spines are so prickly they seem to jump out at you). Make no mistake, this plant is vicious. The tiny barbed hooks on its spines can easily penetrate flesh, and when the victim tries to pull away, the cactus joint often comes with it, digging deeper as the hapless victim struggles to remove it. As irritating as the sharp joints are to most creatures, the desert woodrat uses them to build a home. This small rodent nibbles off the barbed tips of fallen cholla joints and piles them together to build a nest. Although the heavily fortified nest deters a wide range of predators, small snakes sometimes slither through the spines.

Jumping cholla are remarkable desert survivors, able to withstand air temperatures up to 138°F. Most other plants would literally cook at this temperature, but jumping cholla have evolved to withstand intense internal heat.

5 Ocotillo Patch

A mile and a half past the Cholla Cactus Garden, Pinto Basin Road passes through a curvy stretch of road dotted with tall, spindly plants called ocotillo (*Fouquieria splendens*). Often mistaken as a type of cacti, these plants actually belong to a highly unusual family of Mexican trees. Ocotillo is the only member of this family of trees found in the U.S., and its range extends from Southern California into west Texas. It can grow up to 30 feet tall and it's generally found on stony hillsides and alluvial plains.

Ocotillo's long, thorny branches appear dead and grey for most of the year, but they flourish with bright green leaves after it rains. As soon as the leaves appear, the plant photosynthesizes rapidly, storing up as much energy as possible before the soil dries out. When arid conditions return, the leaves fall off and the ocotillo resumes its formerly drab appearance. Although ocotillo can grow green leaves at any time of the year, brilliant red flowers appear on the tips of its branches only in the spring, giving the serpentine plant a fiery touch.

Ocotillo is currently protected by law in both California and Arizona. But it was once a vital resource for people living in the desert. Early settlers' homes were sometimes built from mud-plastered ocotillo limbs, and the thorny stems were planted to make living fences that kept pests out of gardens. Indians used every part of the ocotillo. They burned the branches as firewood, ground the roots into a medicinal powder, and brewed tea from its red blossoms.

7 Cottonwood Spring

This popular destination is home to an easily accessible California fan palm oasis. There's also Cottonwood Visitor Center, which has an information desk, a small store, running water, restrooms, and a small nature trail behind the building. The fan palm oasis is located just below the parking area at the end of the road.

A century ago, Cottonwood Spring gushed over 3,000 gallons a day. Today it pumps out about 500 gallons a day. A few decades ago it barely trickled at all. These drastic fluctuations are the result of shifting water tables, which are determined by the current position of underground faults. As the faults shift during earthquakes, the water table shifts with them, affecting the amount of groundwater that trickles to the surface.

In the days before automobiles and air conditioning, Cottonwood Spring was the only reliable source of water for miles around. Getting here before the heat caught up with you often meant the difference between life and death for desert travelers. A morbid example is the gravesite of Matt Riley, located just north of the Cottonwood Visitor Center. On the morning of July 4, 1905, Riley and a friend set out from the Dale Mining District, 26 miles distant, hoping to reach Cottonwood Spring by sundown. By the time they left, the temperature had already topped 100 degrees. The extreme heat convinced Riley's friend to turn around, but Riley kept on walking, growing more and more dehydrated throughout the day. Shortly before reaching Cottonwood Spring, he collapsed. His shriveled remains were discovered 200 yards from the spring.

᪣ **MASTODON PEAK** ᪥

SUMMARY   This dramatic peak provides sweeping views of the surrounding desert, including the Eagle Mountains, the distant San Jacinto Mountains, and (on clear days) the Salton Sea. The trail to Mastodon Peak starts at Cottonwood Spring and heads southeast for half a mile before reaching a junction. Turn left at the junction (turning right takes you to Lost Palms Oasis), and soon you'll reach the base of Mastodon Peak. A quick scramble up the peak's backside takes you to the top. Mastodon Peak was supposedly named by miners for its vague resemblance to a mastodon. If you're willing to accept that, you can probably also make out Keith Richards, Larry King, and the California Raisins in the folds of the rocks. Just below Mastodon Peak are the remains of the Mastodon Mine, a gold mine that was worked on and off throughout the 1920s. When it first opened, the mine was extremely profitable, but a fault was soon struck and the gold-bearing vein was never relocated. The mine closed for good in 1932.

TRAILHEAD   The trail to Mastodon Peak starts at Cottonwood Springs and heads southeast along a well-marked trail.

◗ **TRAIL INFO** ◗

DIFFICULTY: Strenuous

HIKING TIME: 2 Hours

DISTANCE: 2.5 miles, round-trip

ELEVATION CHANGE: 370 ft.

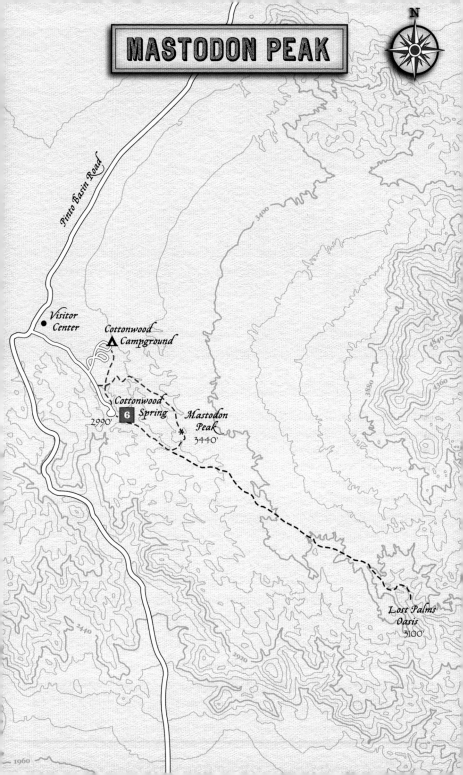

MASTODON PEAK

N

Pinto Basin Road

● Visitor
Center

▲ Cottonwood
Campground

Cottonwood
Spring

2990'

6

✳ Mastodon
Peak
3440'

Lost Palms
Oasis
3100'

3400

4440

3880

4360

1960

2440

2920

Desert fan palms grow up to 75 feet tall and weigh up to three tons. In all of North America, there are only 158 desert fan palm oases—five of which are found in Joshua Tree National Park.

Lost Palms Oasis

29 Palms Inn Restaurant 38
49 Palms Oasis 180
Abandoned Mines 31
Arch Rock 191
Art Galleries 40
Backpacking 21
Barker Dam 133
Barrel Cactus 66
Basics 28
Beavertail Cactus 66
Berdoo Canyon Road 158
Bhakti Fest 41
Bighorn Sheep 76
Biking 27
Birds 74
Bistro 29 38
Black Eagle Mine Road 203
Black Rock 171
Boy Scout Trail 178
Brittlebush 66
Cactus Wren 74
Cahuilla Indians 89
Calico Cactus 66
Campgrounds 32
Camping 30
Canterbury Bells 67
Cap Rock 139
Chia 67
Cholla Cactus Garden 196
Chuckwalla 86
Claret Cup Cactus 67
Coachella Valley 142
Cottonwood Spring 207
Covington Flats 173
Coxcomb Mountains 203
Coyote 78
Coyote Corner 40
Creosote Bush 72
Crossroads Cafe 38
Datura 71
Dehydration 31
Desert Dandelion 67
Desert Institute 30

Desert Mallow 68
Desert Marigold 68
Desert Queen Mine 147
Desert Queen Ranch 129
Deserts 59
Desert Tortoise 80
Desert Washes 204
Desert Willow 68
Dune Primrose 68
Eagle Mountains 203
Ecology 55
Entrance Fees 28
Eureka Peak 173
Festivals 41
Flash Floods 31
Four-Wheel Drive Roads 27
Friends of Joshua Tree 41
Gambel's Quail 74
Geology 47
Geology Tour Road 149
Giant Hairy Scorpion 75
Gold Coin Mine 158
Gold Miners 97
Gram Fest 41
Gram Parsons 119
Hazards 31
Hidden Valley 126
High View Nature Trail 171
Hiking 21
Hiking, Best Hikes 23
History 89
Horseback Riding 27
Hoyt, Minerva 114
Hypothermia 31
Indian Cove 169
Indian Paintbrush 69
Institute For Mentalphysics 37
Integratron, The 44
Introduction 9
Jackrabbit 82
Joshua Tree 37, 62
Joshua Tree Music Festival 41
JTNPA 41

Joshua Tree Outfitters 40
Joshua Tree Roots Music Festival 41
Joshua Tree Saloon 40
Keys, Bill 106
Keys View 142
La Casita Nueva 39
Lang, Johnny 141
Live Oak 162
Lodging 30
Lost Horse Mine 176
Lost Palm Oasis 210
Lucky Boy Vista 147
Malapai Hill 152
Mariposa Lily 69
Mastodon Peak 208
Mojave Aster 69
Mojave Desert 123
Mojave Desert Land Trust 41
Mt. San Jacinto State Park 143
Natural Sisters Cafe 38
Nomad Ventures 40
Notch-leaved Phacelia 69
Oasis of Mara 165
Ocotillo Patch 198
Old Dale Road 203
Palm Springs 143
Pappy & Harriet's 38
Park Rock Cafe 39
Pine City 147
Pinto Basin 194
Pinto Mountains 201
Pioneer Bowl 40
Pioneertown 43
Pleasant Valley 155
Queen Valley 147
Ranger Programs 30
Rattlesnake Canyon 169
Rattlesnakes 84
Restaurants 38
Ricochet 39
Roadrunner 74
Rock Climbing 25
Royal Siam Restaurant 39

Ryan Mountain 174
Saguaro Cacti 195
Salton Sea 144
Sam's Pizza & Indian Food 39
San Andreas Fault 53, 143
Sand Blazing Star 70
Sand Verbana 70
Sand Verbena 70
San Gorgonio Pass 145
San Gorgonio Peak 143
San Jacinto Peak 143
Santana's Mexican Food 39
Serrano Indians 89
Silver Bell Mine 193
Silver Cholla 70
Skull Rock 161
Smallpox 94
Smith's Ranch Drive-in 40
Sonoran Desert 187
South Park Peak 171
Split Rock 162
Squaw Tank 155
Tarantula 75
Tarantula Hawk 75
Teacakes 38
Towns 37
Transverse Mountain Ranges 53
Twentynine Palms 37
U2 118
Visitor Centers 28
Wall Street Mill 134
Warren Peak 182
Weather 29
When to Visit 29
White Tidy-tips 70
Wildflowers 65
Wild West Coyote Fest 41
Willie Boy 101
Wilson Canyon 193
Wonder Garden Cafe 39
Wonderland of Rocks 130
Yucca Man 41
Yucca Valley 37

The Best of the Best

YOSEMITE
• THE COMPLETE GUIDE •

Adventures   Hiking
History   Lodging
Camping   Geology
Wildlife   Backpacking
Waterfalls   High Sierra Camps

YOSEMITE NATIONAL PARK

JAMES KAISER

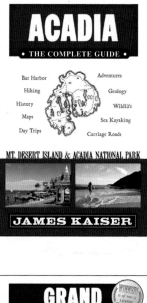

ACADIA
• THE COMPLETE GUIDE •

Bar Harbor   Adventures
Hiking   Geology
History   Wildlife
Maps   Sea Kayaking
Day Trips   Carriage Roads

MT. DESERT ISLAND & ACADIA NATIONAL PARK

JAMES KAISER

JOSHUA TREE
• THE COMPLETE GUIDE •

History   Campgrounds   Nature Trails
Hiking   Maps
Wildflowers   Wildlife
Adventures

JOSHUA TREE NATIONAL PARK

JAMES KAISER

GRAND CANYON
• THE COMPLETE GUIDE •

Adventures
Waterfalls   Lodges
Maps   Wildlife
Hiking   River Trips
Camping

GRAND CANYON NATIONAL PARK

JAMES KAISER

www.jameskaiser.com